I0407300

A Battered Woman's Guide to Victorious Living

by

Janella Purvis

authorHOUSE™

1663 LIBERTY DRIVE, SUITE 200
BLOOMINGTON, INDIANA 47403
(800) 839-8640
WWW.AUTHORHOUSE.COM

© 2005 Janella Purvis. All Rights Reserved.

No part of this book may be reproduced, stored in a retrieval system, or transmitted by any means without the written permission of the author.

First published by AuthorHouse 06/28/05

ISBN: 1-4208-5013-X (sc)

Printed in the United States of America
Bloomington, Indiana

This book is printed on acid-free paper.

This book is in memory of all the women

who lost their lives to domestic violence, &

dedicated to all the women who survived.

Resource Help

If you are in an abusive relationship and need help, call the National Domestic Violence Hotline at

1-800-799-SAFE (7233)

This number can also be used to find out where to get help in your area.

Speaking of Women's Health

The National Speaking of Women's Health Foundation
is dedicated to helping women make informed decisions about their health, well-being, and personal safety. For more information call **1-800-SWH-INFO** or visit the website www. speakingofwomenshealth.com

This program can also be viewed on Lifetime Television at 11:30 a.m./10:30 a.m. Central, Saturdays.

Introduction

The book, A Battered Woman's Guide to Victorious Living is to encourage, empower, and restore the lives of women who are victims of domestic violence. Also helping women find the help and resources they need to create a better life for themselves. Living with an abusive partner creates a dark tunnel of life for the victim that's involved. I've come to tell you that there is a light at the end of the dark tunnel that leads to much success. I want to challenge every reader to put their faith to the test by trusting God and following his directions and he will lead and direct your path. Women of abuse lose all of their self-esteem, character, respect, and passion for life and I want to show you how to get it all back and more!

You don't have to take this treatment, nor do you have to stick around for the long haul! This is a dangerous lifestyle and I want to help every woman realize that she is somebody special and that there is a greater love that no man can give you, and that's the love of God. Living with an abusive partner is like living with a walking time bomb waiting to explode and demolish everything around you. The important thing to know is that it's not the abuser who's so bad, it's the evil spirit that's inside of him that makes him act this way. The seed of abuse was planted in him at childhood and as you read the book you will find out how and why. Women of abuse must realize that they have a choice, don't settle for this lifestyle.

The key to becoming a strong woman is knowing who you are as a woman and as a person. Learning to love yourself and surrounding yourself around positive people and atmospheres will help you get off to a good start. In this book I also encourage women to get a connection with God-Jehovah because he's the main ingredient to becoming a better person and living a better life. Living in an abusive relationship drains you and you need a savior in your life to help rebuild and restore your life back together again. God-Jehovah gives you the strength to leave the abusive relationship and motivates you to doing things you thought you could never do. You can make it and you are somebody special in Gods eyes! It's not a coincidence that you're still here. Girlfriend, you are a survivor and a testimony. You are that light that shines in a tunnel of darkness. Get up from that bed of affliction and shake off the hurt and pain and do something about your life and situation. The ball is in your court so take the first free throw and make a slam dunk out of your life. When your abuser says NO YOU CAN'T, GOD SAYS YES YOU CAN! Read and be blessed and become the women of God that you are suppose to be and gain knowledge that you never had before.

Acknowledgements

I want to thank my Lord and Savior Jesus Christ for being first in my life and blessing me to be able to write this book. For all the times I had writer's block, he stepped in and gave me the words to say. I love this man!

I want to thank my son D.J. because every time I look at him, he gives me the inspiration to keep pushing each and everyday. His little words of inspiration helps me make it through my day. I love you.

My parents, whom I love very much are a great inspiration to me and taught me the importance of working hard and being able to reap the benefits in the end. God bless you both.

Contents

Resources Used

Max Lucado International Study Bible (King James)
Copyright 1995, Word Publishing.

The Holy Bible New King James Version
Copyright 1979,1980,1982 by Thomas Nelson, Inc.

Webster Dictionary 2001

A Battered Woman's Guide
To
Victorious Living.

Ending the torment of Domestic Violence and beginning a life filled with love, joy, peace, and happiness that awaits you.

By:
Janella Purvis

1

THE FIRST BLOW!

Domestic violence is one of the number one killers in today's society as well as emergency room visits by women. This is a very serious and dangerous issue that seems to be taken very lightly by society, the law, and especially the victims of this brutal crime. National Statistics shows that every twelve seconds a woman is beaten by her partner and 52% of female murder victims are killed by their partners. Also children who witness violence in the home are 74% more likely to commit assault. I'm sure the percentage rate will change by the time you read this book. This is a situation that has gone extremely out of hand. The victims of domestic violence are afraid to fight back or escape the situation because they fear for their lives. If you are a victim of this brutal crime, don't just sit around in fear and do nothing. You need to get help, seek professional counseling, and if all else fails, leave the abusive partner before tragedy strikes. If your partner refuses to get help, then you get help and leave him alone because obviously he's not willing to change.

There's power in the fist that goes way beyond the actual hitting. It sucks the life out of your spirit and devours your energy, causing you not to function properly. Every **blow** received, leaves a bruise that damages your self-esteem, self-respect, and your inner spirit. You will find it hard to relate and interact with others. Every **blow** plants a negative seed into your life and spirit. Instead of a blooming tree filled with lively fruit, all you have is a lifeless tree full of dead roots, dead weeds and dry leaves that produces rotten fruit! Whatever is inside of you will come out of you. If negativity has been planted into your spirit then negativity will come out of you. Your abuser has beaten you to the point where you have no love, joy, peace, happiness, or self-esteem. You have just accepted the fact that you are what your abuser says you are and you will be what he says you will be.

The **first blow** is the gift that keeps on giving, the more you receive freely, the more will be given unto you. The best thing to do is to stop it before it gets started. After receiving the first hit, make it known to your abuser that there will be no more beatings! Just like a wild animal can sense, feel, and smell the presence of fear, so can the abuser. Once he sees you're afraid, he will start preying on that fear and torture you for as long as you allow him to. The **first blow** is usually a hard hit on the head that can damage all kinds of nerve cells and destroy proper functioning in the brain. The abuser wants to get inside your head to destroy your thought pattern and brainwash you into thinking like him and once he's in your head, he knows he's got you! He wants you to get amnesia, a loss of memory so you can't remember anything that's positive about yourself, only the negative to destroy you mentally and physically.

Take a few moments and ask yourself these questions. When did you receive your **first blow?** Why did it happen? Where did it happen? What could **you** have done to prevent it from happening? I know it's hard to think back to the first time you've been beaten by your mate, you may feel like you're reliving that dreadful day all over again. This process will help you find solutions to your abusive problems and begin to help you walk in healing and total deliverance. When a man hits you for the very first time, you're filled with mixed emotions and you think to yourself, maybe he just had a hard day at work or just stressed. You may even begin feeling you're at fault and begin blaming yourself and being apologetic. Also feeling bitter and resentful and retaliating in the wrong way at the wrong time. Or you can allow the spirit of fear to come upon you and do nothing which is definitely the wrong thing to do!

2

The questions may arise like, how can he hit me if he says he loves me? How can he speak to me this way and disrespect me in this manner if he loves me? You really don't know why it happened, all you know is that it did and thankful that you're still alive to tell the story! When you finally get the courage to ask your abuser why did he hit you, the response is always; **YOU MADE ME DO IT AND YOU NEEDED TO BE TAUGHT A LESSON!** First of all what's the lesson that's suppose to be learned here? You already have one father rather he raised you or not, and you don't need two! The truth is he really doesn't love you if he beats you nor does he respect you if he calls you every bad name under the sun! I don't care what you've done or how bad it was, you don't deserve to be hit under any circumstance. If you do something he doesn't like, you're suppose to be able to sit down and talk about it together and come to an agreement. He uses you as his punching bag to help him release stress, and that's not fair to you. He knows he can't walk around punching anyone else and get away with it, so he comes home to you because he knows you will take it! Sometimes, it's hidden anger in him that has nothing to do with you, it's the spirit inside of him, he's like a walking time bomb waiting to explode. It's important not to focus so much on the abuser that you lose focus on the spirit that's within him. Don't get me wrong, it's ok to be angry with the situation, but you must do a little research to find out why your abuser is so violent. Do a background check, find out where he picked up such a bad habit from! Men are human and make mistakes, but sometimes we hate the man and should be hating the demonic spirit that's inside of him! The seed of abuse may have been planted in him as a child growing up by watching his parents fight. Being exposed to this type of behavior may be all that he knows, even though it's wrong, he feels it's right because that's what he saw his father do to his mother. In fact the National Statistics shows that more than half the children who are boys that witness their fathers beating their mothers more likely become batterers. Now this isn't always the case, sometimes the abuser just wants to have control and wants to boss everyone around and when he can't have his way, he retaliates with violence!

Not to make excuses for men, but they go through so much stress in their personal lives, financially, and with society. A lot of men can't handle great amounts of pressure and stress. When they come home-that's their castle, the only place where they feel welcome, comfortable and like a king! They don't have to bow down to the boss on the job or deal with unwanted issues, just lay back and relax. Now ladies, we are known for having a **nagging spirit**! If you know how your man is and what makes him go-off then you should know what lines not to cross. Don't nag him about silly things like not taking out the trash, walking the dog, not picking up his socks out of the floor, etc. I mean don't get me wrong, these are things that will get on your nerves to no limit, but it's not worth starting a heated argument that will cause you to get the worst end of the bargain. Make home life as comfortable as possible for the both of you. I'm not saying suck-up to him, but keep peace-please! If you know what makes him tick, by all means don't do it. If you know what makes beast come out, don't provoke him. All I'm saying is, if you know your man is violent and you know his normal routine of how he acts when he's on the edge, don't provoke him. Just keep your distance until he's in a better mood and has gotten over his fit! Whatever issues you have with him, wait and discuss them when he's in a peaceful mood, observe his mood before approaching him.

I remember as a child growing up, my grandparents would fight like cats and dogs. My grandmother was a big 380lb woman and my grandfather was a little short skinny bow-legged man who weighed about 160lbs. It didn't matter the size at all, they would fight until one or the other gave in. I remember being terrified to death, they were old and I couldn't do anything to stop them from fighting. All I could do was just cry and hope that they didn't kill each other. But grandma knew how my grandpa was, he was little but he had a bad temper and she knew him like a book from cover-to-cover and spine-to spine! Grandma knew every Thursday was their day to fight. Grandpa would come home from work every Thursday in a horrible mood and as soon as he would come in the house, he would deliberately start an argument with grandma so he could jump on her and start fighting her. So grandma got smart, it became a routine for her, so every Thursday, she was ready for the showdown as soon as he walked through the door, she was ready.

They got married when they were fifteen years old and was fighting from all of those years into old age. In fact, I think the last time I remember seeing them fight was when they were in their mid-sixty's and that is too old to be fighting anybody. They fought all of those years and it effected them, their children and grandchildren. My grandparents, may they rest in peace, planted negative seeds into their six children's lives as well as grandchildren. When violence is all you see and experience, that's all you know! I grew up thinking that a woman was suppose to be beaten if she messed up, until I found out the truth through experience. This is a family curse that's been passed down from generation to generation, and needs to be broken and is already broken starting with me and my son. Just like my grandma learned the routine of my grandpa's violent ways, a lot of you ladies are doing the same thing, you have developed a pattern and allowed yourselves to become used to your man's violent ways by accepting them and doing nothing about it. You know when he's coming home and what he's going to do when he gets there-even the day and time he's going to come and beat the crap out of you too!

This is no game, it's serious, even though my grandma won most of the fights, who's to say that you will win all of yours or live to tell your story. My grandmother knew that it wasn't her strength, it was God's powerful grace and mercy that saw her through all of those tough years of abuse. She even admitted that she would pray for God to cover and protect her before my grandpa came home from work. Grandma didn't believe in divorce or separation, so she stayed in that violent marriage for years. My grandparents were married almost seventy years. It was the Lord that delivered them both from their violent ways and gave them the strength to stay together for all of those years. Even though my grandparents got saved and delivered from that mess, the spirits transferred to their sons! My grandparents had six children - five boys and one girl. All of them grew up with bad tempers and violent ways! When the sons got married, they treated their wives the same way they saw their father do their mother when they were young boys. They thought women were beneath them and should obey their every command and when they didn't, they retaliated with violence. Then the violent curse was passed down from the five sons to their sons who also were violent to their companions. As I said before domestic violence is the gift that keeps on giving until put to an end. That's why it's important to look beyond the abuser and his attitude, and find out exactly what's the story behind his violent ways and try to help him open up more and seek help.

So many men go through hurt and disappointment from childhood on to adulthood and just need someone to talk to and understand them. They want to act as though they're so tough and nothing bothers them, but inside they are crying out for love and understanding. Now ladies, be understanding, but don't be foolish! It's important to find out the background of your man, but don't allow him to use this as a weapon to play with your emotions and use his childhood issues as a guilt trip to make you stay in an abusive relationship. Don't become a slave to this brutal crime and become a prisoner in your own home. Slaves lived in constant fear for their lives daily, wondering if the master was pleased with their works and if not, how severe would the punishment be. A slave has no freedom of speech or choice in their own lives, it's all directed by the master! Slaves are also brainwashed into thinking that they're nothing, nobody loves or cares about them and that there's no way out. There is a path for escape, you just have to decide which path you'll take, the path of destruction or the path of deliverance! Like the former slave, Harriet Tubman broke free from the bondage of slavery and helped other slaves break free, so can you! Don't settle for this lifestyle, this isn't love- when someone loves you, they don't hurt you. There may be power in the fist but there is a greater power in God and through his love, you can break free from the bondages of physical abuse!

2

STOP, LOOK, LISTEN, AND GO !

<u>STOP!</u>

There is so much going on around you right now that you don't know your right foot from your left! You're walking around all confused, not realizing that everything around you is falling apart as well as yourself. You need to grab hold of yourself and get in touch with reality as well as getting your house and life in order. This is the time where you need to just **stop** everything you're doing and get in touch with your surroundings. You've allowed the enemy-Satan to attack you long enough and destroy everything that you've worked so hard to accomplish. I know this is a hard pill to swallow but, if you are still allowing yourself to go through daily torment and abuse from your mate, then you've allowed the enemy-Satan to take control and he now has the power!

Ladies, it's important to remember that Satan has no power over you or your mate unless it's given to him or room is made for him to dwell in your temple. Remember, it's not your mate as a person that's so bad, it's the spirit of Satan that has entered his temple (body) that is causing all of the havoc! So from the head on down to you and your kids, if you have any, are being destroyed by this evil spirit.

Once you decide to put a **stop** to this madness, you will gain control over your life and the things around you.

After you've taken full inventory over your life and surroundings you must begin to count up the costs and the losses and do what's needed to regain fullness again. You don't have strength alone, it's God-Jehovah that gives you the strength to move on and make a change. Once you put an end to the abuse and all other nonsense going on in your life, God will strengthen and motivate you to a new level of greatness. You will no longer care about how others perceive you. Read chapter Psalm 121 for instruction on seeking God.

> *Psalm 121*
> *5v) The Lord is your keeper; The Lord is your shade at your right hand.*
> *7v) The Lord shall preserve you from all evil; He shall preserve your soul.*
> *8v) The Lord shall preserve your going out and coming in from this time forth, and even forever more.*

LOOK!

Now that you have stopped to get yourself together, now it's time to take a long **look** at yourself in the mirror and ask yourself some serious questions. Do you like what you see? Do you like what you've become? Have you become blinded to the reality of life? It's no longer about the abuser anymore or what he or anyone else thinks about you, it's all about you honey! When you look into the mirror if you see an ugly face filled with fear, bruises, scars, depression and tears- that's a sign that a spiritual make-over needs to take process. Reality has finally set in, you are no longer satisfied with the person that you've become in looks and attitude. Your mind has been filled with so much junk that you began to believe what the enemy has been telling you.

A person is always affected by what they see in one way or the other. If you see an old picture of yourself as a child, and you were fat, that picture affected you in some way and made you want to lose weight so you can be healthy. If you see that both of your parents suffer from high blood pressure and all kinds of diseases run in your family- then you will want to eat right and take better care of yourself because you see how your family is suffering with the disease. If you are suffering from physical abuse or domestic violence and you begin to see how it's affecting you and your kids (if you have any) then you want to begin to make a change to make things better for yourself.

The eyes are the lamp of the body, if they are blinded by darkness, then you can't see. The problem with a lot of women who are victims of domestic violence, is that we allow the truth that we see to be covered in darkness. Sin is darkness and it's a sin for a woman not to take care of herself and to hide the truth. Battered Women want to hide the fact that they are getting they're brains knocked-out daily! You don't want anybody to know because you are ashamed but more so afraid. The enemy-Satan has led you to believe that your abuser loves you and is only beating you in love and you deserve to be treated like a slave! The devil is a liar and the truth is not in him!

The cataracts need to be removed from your eyes so that you may see the truth for what it really is. The devils dust has been kicked in your eyes and has blinded you from the truth. The eyes lead you to where you are going and shows you light, truth, and reality. Your life has been contaminated with lies and deceit and you've been made to feel that there is nothing better in store for you and to just settle for less but as I said before- the devil is a liar! In the bible the 11th chapter of the book of Luke discusses the eye being the lamp of the body and that when the eye is good, the whole body is good but when the eye is bad the body is filled with darkness. Don't allow your eyes to be blinded any longer with deceit. Pray and ask God for spiritual guidance and to help you be able to see the truth! Repeat this prayer with me.

Father God in the mighty name of Jesus, remove the cataracts from my eyes, so I can see people, places, and things for what and who they really are. Give me the strength to deal with the hurt and pain that I've experienced, give me a forgiving heart so that I can love everyone-even the ones who have done me wrong. Take me out of the darkness of sin, wash me up and forgive me

for all my wrong-doing. **Create in me a clean heart and renew the contrite spirit in me, and make me be the strong woman of God that you will have me to be. Save my mind, heart, body, soul and spirit for I want to be like your son, Jesus Christ- holy, pure, and righteous. My temple is empty right now God, please fill me with godliness, forgiveness, and positivity. Most of all help me to be able to move on higher in the things of God by your divine direction. Amen.**

Read the 11ᵗʰ Chapter of Luke beginning with the 33ʳᵈ verse about the lamp of the body, which is your eye. These verses will help you understand more and more as to how important it is to see, not only in the natural but in the spiritual realm as well. Make sure your eyes are no longer focused in the things of darkness but the things of light. Begin to look at yourself in a different light and you and your situations will change.

Luke Chapter 11
33v) No one, when he has lit a lamp, puts it in a secret place or under a basket, but on a lamp stand, that those who come in may see the light.
34v) The lamp of the body is the eye. Therefore, when your eye is good, your whole body also is full of light. But when your eye is bad, your body also is full of darkness.
35v) Therefore take heed that the light which is in you is not darkness.
36v) If then your whole body is full of light, having no part dark, the whole body will be full of light, as when the bright shining of a lamp gives you light.

LISTEN!

The word **listen** means to hear and to pay attention. What words are you hearing being spoken to you? Are they words of love, words of hate, or negative words that you're allowing to be deposited into your spirit? Words of love brings forth life, touches the heart, and causes it to beat in harmony. Words of hate damages the heart and brings forth a slow death by slowing down the heart beat that loses harmony to your soul. Now this isn't a physical death- but more so a spiritual death because words of hate can kill your dreams, self-esteem, and the liveliness that you once felt from within. Negative words spoken to you brings forth a negative view as to how you think and feel about yourself. You begin to question yourself and become judgemental on everything and everyone around you.

It's very important to pay attention to what's being said to you. You don't always have to respond to what the person is saying, but just pay attention and take heed to the words being spoken. A person can learn a lot about someone or something if they just observe and listen to what's being said and done. For example, if you have a friend and all he or she does is lie, you don't have to let them know that you know they're lying- just observe and pay attention to what's being said and he or she will tell on themselves without even realizing it. You see, a pathological liar will talk all over themselves and forget the previous lie that they told before. That's why it's vital to **listen** to every word that is spoken out of the mouths of others as well as yourself.

Ladies, it's very important to know who you are as a person and have that inner-strength abiding in you daily. If you don't know who you are and don't have a positive view of yourself, you can easily be destroyed by the enemy who's tormenting you. Even the strongest, most positive person can be affected by negative words and surroundings. You can be the most upbeat positive person in the world but if you surround yourself around negative people and atmospheres-you will also begin to act, think, and feel like them. Observe the people you hang around and your atmospheres, is there a spirit of peace, love, and joy or a spirit of jealousy, envy, strife and much havoc?!? Is your mate depositing positive or negative energy into your spirit?

The abuser can't find anything good to say about you because he doesn't have anything good to say about himself, really. He's under a lot of pressure on the job and he knows he can't throw his weight around there, so he waits until he comes home to do it. He feels threatened by you because you're walking around all positive and he's mad because you're happy and he's not. You're going to work everyday, coming home and doing more work, making sure the house is in order, making sure the kids are taken care of and he feels that he's not needed. A man loves to feel needed. If he doesn't feel needed his ego is torn down and that's when the madness really begins, but only for the weak brothers who don't know who they are. The pressures of life has given him a raw deal. He wants to take it out on someone that will take the punches, won't fight back and willing to take the verbal abuse without speaking up for themselves in return!

The abuser is observing you and wants to figure out a way he can break you down. So he says to himself; I know how I can get her, I 'll tell her she's fat, ugly, and doesn't please me anymore. I'll tell her she's stupid and no one will want her, so she might as well stay with me because I'm the best thing she'll ever have! And once he get's into your mind, he's got you right where he wants you. He's studied and observed you long enough to know where your strengths and weaknesses are. The abuser has figured out where to hit you at the hardest with negative words and painful punches to break you down! Does this sound formiliar?

I know what it feels like to be called names like stupid, fat, ugly, whore, bitch, etc. Especially from someone that says they love you and will never do or say anything to hurt you. I was in a relationship for six long years with a man and only two years out of the six were good! He was a true thug, but I didn't try to change him, I loved him for who he was. The problem was he didn't know what love was or how to love-he was afraid to open up to me. To make a long story short, before I met him I was usually always a positive upbeat person and felt good about myself. I was very independent, always worked two jobs to maintain and always kept money in the bank. I needed him for love, not money. There was nothing he could give me that I couldn't get for myself!

I was told that I was too independent and controlling, the point is when my ex-boyfriend saw that I wasn't dependent on him, he became intimidated. He tried to figure out a way to break me down so I could depend on no one but him. Needless to say, he finally found a way to break me down and that was by attacking my strongest points. Even the strongest person can become weak if not careful!

See he knew I always took pride in my appearance, so he started calling me fat, ugly, and finding everything else wrong with me. He knew I was kind of shy so he would wait until company would come around the house and call me a stupid bitch, crazy, and try to call me out to make himself look good! I always had money saved, he deliberately stopped helping me pay bills so I could spend all of my money that I had saved in the bank and it worked! I never waited on him to give his half of the bill money, I just paid the bills myself because I always liked paying bills on time.

The point I want to make is, he observed and studied my character and knew my strengths and weaknesses. The more he called me fat, ugly, and stupid the more I began to believe it. No matter how strong of a person I thought I was, he was still able to break me down with those cruel words. I began to bring life to every negative word spoken to me and allowed myself to become exposed to this junk every single day of my life! If you surround yourself around negative people, you will become what they are. I was surrounded by a negative person who didn't even love himself, so I became the same way and began to believe that I was the person he said I was because there was no one else around to tell me any different. That's why it's vital that you surround yourself around positive people that will speak positive words into your life.

There is a better life for the battered woman, you don't have to settle for less! You not only have a battle with your abuser, but also a battle with the flesh and spirit! During this battle you will hear the voice of Satan and the voice of God Jehovah speaking to you. If you have no connection or relationship with God Jehovah, you won't know his voice when he's speaking to you. God will tell you things you don't want to hear, things to help you grow, speak words into your life to make you become a better person even if it hurts sometimes. When Satan speaks to you, he will tell you what you want to hear, especially when he knows it's what you really want to do and your emotions are all tangled up in your flesh! But he can also make you feel less of yourself by speaking negative words into your life like; you are a loser, you will never make it, no one loves you or believes in you and you will never have the victory!

The voice of God is what you should be listening to, the voice that says you can make it, you are a survivor, you are loved, you are somebody, you can and will make a difference in this world, and most of all victorious in all you do! The voice that says you've had enough, you don't have to settle for this kind of treatment, and you can escape and come out on top with your hands up! These are the words that you long to here and God will speak these words into your life, only if you have the **listening ear** to receive them. God knows and sees all things, good and bad and wants to bring you out of the mess that you're in. Once you've done all that you know how to do to make the relationship work and things still aren't changing, it's time to go! Wait for God to give you instructions on what to do, don't move unless he tells you to. When you move by the power of God and by his divine instructions, you won't be out of order. Learn to listen to the voice of God and follow his path. Now that you've **stopped, looked, and listened** it's now time to pack your bags and **go!**

GO!

Please don't misunderstand me, I'm not encouraging women to leave their spouses, if you can work it out, by all means please do it! But this is for the women who have done all they can do to make things better and the abuser just simply refuses to change. Before I go any further, the only way to work out an abusive relationship is to seek God Jehovah and both parties be willing to work together to change for the better. It takes two to destroy a relationship but it takes three to build it back together again and that's God, the man and the woman. The word **go** means to leave, move away, or depart. Battered Woman, you've reached that point in your life where you have to make a very important decision on whether you're going to stay or go!

It's time that you start looking at yourself as being more than a punching bag, don't allow yourself to live in misery, fear, and discomfort any longer! It's time to step out of the box and live a peaceful life filled with freedom and love. Of course, you know that the enemy-Satan is going to do everything in his power to keep you bound in misery and tell you all of the things that you can't do or accomplish on your own. He's going to remind you every chance he gets that you'll never make it or survive without a man in your life. The very moment, he realizes that you're thinking about leaving, he's going to cause your abuser to start acting really nice and all lovey-dovey! Then your mind and emotions get all confused and you say to yourself, maybe I'll stay and give him one more chance. The devil will use the abuser to give you everything you want and feed your head and heart full of lies and then move in for the kill!

Your abuser's mind is very weak and has been programmed to do whatever Satan tells him to do. If he's told to act nice, he will and if he's told to curse you out, he will and if he's told to kill you he will do also because he's the enemy's slave! That's why it's vital for you to get out of the situation you're in because tragedy can strike at anytime and it can be avoided if you hearken unto the voice of God Jehovah and move by his power and demand. Victims of abuse procrastinate too much! Don't waste time messing around with foolishness, get up and do something now before its too late! This is your life on the line, you can either lose it or save it, the choice is yours. If your abuser is very possessive, violent, paranoid and has already threatened to kill you, don't tell him you're leaving, let's not be crazy! If you tell him, you'll never make it out alive or in one peace. Instead, wait until he's not at home or ask a police officer to escort you to your property to get your things. The final words of this chapter is to **go** in Jesus Name and enter a new life filled with bountiful blessings.

3

NEW BEGINNINGS!

You have gone through so many trials and tribulations in your life and you wonder how did you ever make it out alive and on top. You were once in a low place in life called the valley that was filled with depression, hurt, pain, confusion, low self-esteem and brokeness. Now that you've climbed out of the valley of a lowly place, you can begin to feel the power of God moving in your life and taking you to higher dimensions in him. Don't waste your time dwelling on the things that happened yesterday, for yesterday is gone and we can't bring it back and shouldn't want to! Learn how to thank God for where you are today. Just think about how far he's brought you and how long he's kept you from all hurt, harm, danger, evil, wickedness, sickness, and death. I guarantee you'll begin to praise him for where you are right now! You should just stop reading right now and take a praise break and shout Hallelujah!

It's not a coincidence that you made it this far, God Jehovah has a plan and destiny for your life that you must fulfill. The devil couldn't kill you because God spoke life and not death to you and your situation. Now, for the ladies reading this book who don't have a relationship with Jesus Christ, you really need to get to know him personally and intimately as your savior. If you don't, you will never understand where he's trying to take you in your life and spirit. Without the Lord in your life you have no direction nor fulfillment, you're just lost and empty inside. Fear can easily step in and tell you all of the things you can't do and places you can't go if you have no spiritual direction. It's time for new beginnings in your life, you're free from your past and now you're ready for full restoration and divine direction to walk into your destiny.

Starting over can be very challenging, but you must be willing to make sacrifices to improve your life and the things around you. You are no longer living your life the way your ex-abuser told you to live it, but the way you want to. Begin to prioritize your life by making things easier and changing the way you do things, the way you look at things, even the way you handle certain situations. Also make sure you put the things that are most important first and handle your business affairs promptly. Another good way to start over is by relocating. Sometimes it's good to get away from friends and family and all of the people, places, and things that are trying to hold you back from moving forward into your destiny. Staying in the same environment brings forth constant reminders of your past and makes it hard to focus properly on the things which are ahead.

It's also very important to keep your personal plans to yourself, don't be so quick to tell your business to friends and family. Sometimes family can be more harm to you than good, by offering you terrible advice and opinions of what you should and shouldn't do. They're on the outside looking into your situation, but totally clueless as to what is really going on. Don't allow anyone to encourage you to stay in a violent relationship. There is no way of working it out when your brains and teeth are being knocked out all over the place, ok! You will always have that negative, unforgiving friend who always wants to bring up the past and not willing to forgive your abuser for what he's done. You will also have that nosey family member who wants to keep up with what you're doing and where you're going, so they can work against you. In their hearts they think they are helping you and your situation but in actuality they are hurting you. They always want to offer unhelpful and unwanted advice. That's why it's important to keep your personal business to yourself, in situations like abuse, you don't know who to trust.

Let me share a story with you about a lady who lived in my neighborhood... let's just say her name was Sharon. Anyway, her husband used to beat her up almost everyday, he would get arrested and a few days later come right back home and do the same thing again. Sharon was a very smart, independent, talented and beautiful lady. She had all kinds of bachelor and master degrees- the woman had it going on until she got hooked up with the wrong man. Her husband was very jealous and he wasn't the most finest man walking the streets, if you know what I mean. He knew Sharon didn't need him for anything but love, he began to feel very intimidated-almost like a shadow hiding behind her. People always put Sharon high up on a pedestal and praised her for her works and contributions to the communities. This made her husband furious because he felt disrespected and ignored.

According to Sharon he was a great lover and was good with fixing things around the house. Besides all of that he had no education and no money-he basically lived off of Sharon's wealth. Now don't get me wrong, he had a job but he didn't make enough to pay the most expensive bills and this was one of the main things that bothered him. So he began to take out his frustrations on Sharon and beat her until he made himself feel satisfied! He would even brag about how he made her yell and scream, he actually thought this was funny! He felt that if he beat her, he could get back at her for how she made him feel less than a man. Sharon loved him, but I must admit she was one of those who did try to make him feel beneath her in public and tear down his ego! A man's ego is one thing you don't mess with, once they lose their ego, that's it! So he felt like he was hiding behind Sharon's shadow, felt intimidated by her beauty and success, and his ego was basically destroyed! He loved her but he became jealous, possessive, violent, and paranoid, he had to know her every move.

One night her husband beat her up so bad-he knocked out five of her teeth in one blow and then chased her out of the house naked! The reason for this fight to this day is unknown but he tried to beat the beauty out of her and did a great job of it too! Every time she tried to run away, you could hear him grab her and throw her against the wall, he then later got a gun and chased her out of the house. Well, she ran to a neighbors house for help and he threatened the neighbors that he would shoot the door down if they didn't let him in. They called the cops and they took their sweet time about coming but needless to say, they came. Sharon's neighbors let her spend the night and while her darling hubby was taken to jail, Sharon decided to escape. She went to go live with her brother who lived in another city and state, she figured her husband would never find her there. After all Sharon and her brother barely spoke-they weren't enemies, they just weren't close.

To make a long story short, Sharon had been living with her brother for about three months and doing well until her nosey aunt decided to interfere. She kept telling Sharon that she needed to try to work things out with her husband and to pray for his change as well as telling her that it was her fault that he was abusing her. Well, this made Sharon furious, she's walking around with about five teeth missing from the front of her mouth and her aunt is telling her she's the blame for what happened to her. Of course, you know Sharon had to read her aunt really quick! She went off and told her aunt that she needs to mind her business and that she was never going back to her husband again. Well this news didn't set too well with her aunt, so aunty decided to take matters into her own hands and went to talk to the husband who had no idea where Sharon was at the time. In her aunts mind she was helping but later discovers she made the wrong choice.

One day Sharon was alone at her brothers house and she got a surprise visit from her husband, he put his hand over her mouth and told her not to scream or he would kill her! He told her that her darling aunty told him where she was and that he needed to come and get her and work things out. When Sharon told him she wasn't coming back, he snapped and beat her so bad that she had to be hospitalized for months. He beat her and left her there in a pool of blood, her sister-in-law came home from work early and found the door wide opened, she walked in and found Sharon lying on the floor covered in blood! He damaged several nerve cells in her brain and she now walks with a limp. I told you all of this to show you the dangers of having friends and family all in your business, you think they have your best interest at heart but they are ready to stab you right in your heart!

Please take heed to the stories that I'm sharing with you in this book. Don't be like Sharon- once beautiful and had it going on and now she's walking around with a limp, disabled, and has a nervous condition. This could've been prevented if her nosey aunt would've stayed out of her business and not intervened. Sharon's life was almost lost, even though she's not in the best condition, thank God she's alive and her husband is where he should be, jail! The lesson I want you to get from this is to know who you are as a powerful woman and when you make the choice to move on with your life, don't allow others such as family and friends to dictate to you what you should do and how you should do it! It's your life and you can keep it, if you let the Lord lead you, not your nosey family members and friends! That's why I'm encouraging every woman that's looking for a way out to seek the source-God Jehovah and he'll show you an exit. If you want a better life and a change of atmosphere, you need to move to a better area, find a better job and most of all get into a good church that preaches and teaches the true word of God so you won't lose your fire, focus, or direction!

Another important lesson in starting your new life is to not look back. You have made it through the struggle and now it's time to breathe again. When you lose something the first thing you do is think back to where you last had the object. The second thing you do is to turn around and go back to all of the places where you remember having the object at and try to find it. When you lose or miss something, you have a choice as to rather you will go back for it or just forget about it and move on. It usually depends on the value of the object as to rather you will go back for it or not. The words I want you to focus on here is, **going back**. You can never have new beginnings in your life if you're always going back to your past and reliving those painful memories. Don't continue to think about the hell you've gone through, just focus on your brand new life filled with joy and peace. The dangers of looking back is that it will cause you to go back to your old self again and the next thing you know, you'll be home-sweet-home again getting the life knocked out of you! There is danger in looking back because when you're looking back, you must turn around. In turning around, you must look back and if what you're looking back at entices your eyes and spirit, you've then fallen into the trap of temptation.

The only thing that you should be tempted to fall into are the things of God and his blessings. Whatever you want to do, do it in Jesus Name, wherever you want to go, go in Jesus Name, and whatever you want to be, strive to be it in Jesus Name- fake it until you make it baby! The important thing to remember is that you have to know that the Lord is with you at all times. When you're operating under the direction of the Lord you can easily be assured that he's got you covered and you don't have to be afraid anymore and can live in comfort. After a hard fall in life, you must take your time and take things one day at a time. My advice to any woman starting over in life is to yield to the Lord. This book isn't about religion and I don't want to offend anyone by any means, but God Jehovah is the only one that can help you get your life back on track. Salvation is the key, your life needs to be put into the hands of someone who really cares and has the power to destroy your enemies and everything that's working against you.

4

LEARNING TO LOVE YOURSELF AND OTHERS

Now that you have chosen to leave your past behind and start over again, you must be able to adjust to the new life and the new you. In the beginning it can all seem very foreign or strange to you. It's hard trying to adjust to the new single lifestyle when you're so used to having someone around. It can also be very hard moving to a different town and leaving all of your friends and family behind you. But in the midst of all of the new changes in your life, you must be able to accept them as they come and be able to cope with what lies ahead of you. It doesn't matter what happens or what is going on around you, you must be happy with yourself and the changes around you. If you aren't happy then everything and everyone around you will be miserable and unhappy as well.

In this chapter I want to discuss learning how to love yourself and others. If you love yourself then it will be easy for others to love you. Love has no color, it's so innocent and pure. When you look at yourself in the mirror, do you see a woman who's heart is filled with love and peace or a woman who's heart is still filled with hurt, anger, hatred, and pain? When you see a man how does your heart and emotions feel toward him? Does your heart become hardened and bitter toward every man you see? Or is your heart open to receive love and give love back? These are questions you must ask yourself and hopefully find answers and solutions to. It's sad when you don't know who you are and even worse when you don't love yourself and others around you.

When your heart has been hurt by someone it means that it's been damaged in some way. When your heart has been hurt and damaged it becomes defected. A defected heart can't function properly, it's not strong as it used to be, nor can it take the bumps and bruises as it used to. A strong heart can take anything because its in proper function and has no defects, but a weak heart is very sensitive. For example some people are very soft-hearted, you have to be careful what you say to them because they are so sensitive and take everything negatively to heart. But a strong-hearted person or a hard-hearted person can take anything, it doesn't effect them. Why? Because they know who they are as a person and they don't allow people to feed their heart with negative junk. They don't allow the thoughts, words, and views of others enter their minds and hearts. You have to know who you are and guard your heart from negative people and things. Guard your heart with love, words of inspiration and the word of God.

Learning to love yourself is easy, don't make it hard. All you have to do is search within yourself and ask God to release you from the hurt and pain that you are feeling in your heart and whoever and whatever that is trying to attack it. You should no longer look in the mirror at yourself and see the old soul who was once beaten, bruised, and scorned. You should be able to see yourself as a brand new soul that's full of fire and desire to live her life free in Jesus and in all things. Look forward to what is coming ahead in your life. In due timing God will send someone special in your life that will love you for you and except the good, the bad, and the ugly. But not until he completes his surgery on you and your heart. Right now your heart has a four-corner brick wall around it, your guard is up so high that you're afraid to take it down. I understand completely, when you've been hurt, you try to protect the things that are most precious to you. But in order for God to heal your heart, you must allow him to tear down those walls that you've built around your stoney heart.

Once God has access to your heart, he can take out all of the defects such as hurt, pain, hatred, jealousy, envy, strife and unforgiveness. He can make your oversized heart filled with junk from your past, the right size again and change the irregular heartbeat into beating in the right tune. God wants to give you a brand new heart and fill it with his love, power, and strength so you can love yourself as well as others. There should no longer be a guard around your heart keeping you from loving and receiving love. In fact, the only guard that you should have around your heart is the one that God has given you. God will protect your heart from the snares of the enemy, the bullets from Satan himself, and anything or anyone that tries to fill it with negativity. God closes the door to your heart that no man shall be able to open without an access code. God only gives a person the combination to your heart that is worthy.

When God has completed his surgical operation on your heart, you will know it, because you can love the people who have hurt you and have spitefully misused you. You can love people who have lied on you and scandalized your name, you can have compassion and forgiveness for the ones who have wronged you in the past and present. You will be able to look at yourself in the mirror and smile and be happy with who you are and who God has made you to be. Be happy with your big lips, big eyes, short hair, long legs, long arms, big nose, dark skin/light skin, big feet/short feet, big butt/flat butt, voluptuous breasts or droopy breasts! It doesn't matter what you have or don't have, it's the way God made you and you must learn to be happy and content with who you are in Christ and as a woman of greatness. There is no such thing as an ugly woman. God said in his word that everything he made was good and wonderfully made in his image. Now, no matter what you may think you look like or what flaws you may have, you are beautiful and perfect in Gods eyes.

Once you have accepted the way you are as a better person in Christ, you can learn to love everything about yourself. You can look at yourself everyday in the mirror and thank God for the way he created you in his image. Give yourself a big hug every morning and tell yourself how much you love yourself and how good you look. You may not be happy with your appearance, but ask God to give you what you need and to teach you how to make yourself look and feel beautiful. I don't care even if you are depressed, tell yourself everyday that you are beautiful and a winner in all things in life. The more you say it, the more you will believe it and bring birth to those positive words spoken over your life.

It's important to speak those things that be not, as though they were. Don't consider it as lying or wishful thinking. For example you can look, dress, and act like a millionaire but not even have one penny to your name. You can look and dress like a homeless person on the street but be filthy rich! You can pretend like your marriage is going so great in public, but behind closed doors you are really going through a storm. The point is that you know your real situation isn't all that great, but you have to speak against the attack of the enemy-Satan by speaking faith-filled words to your present situation to bring death to Satan's plan to destroy you, your family, and finances.

Ladies, I know you've gone through hell and back, but you are determined that you are going to live a better life for yourselves and your family. You may have some permanent bruises and scars from your abusive relationships that show on your face and body, but that doesn't mean that you can't fix it with makeup, surgery or hide it with clothing accessories. There is always a way out of anything if you trust and believe in God. God wants you to see the real you that's hiding behind the scenes. He wants that scared little girl that's inside you to come out and play! Enjoy your life and focus on the love that awaits you. There is no love like God's love and once you have experienced his love and realize that he loves you just the way you are, you can love yourself and others around you.

Don't continue to look at the battered woman who's face is full of bruises and scars in the mirror. Look at the new resurrected woman of God who's burdens have been lifted and who's mind, heart, and spirit has now been renewed and changed forever. Be loosed to love again, but it all starts with you loving God, and yourself. Your past died when you left the abuse and started a new life. Your present future is now alive because you have found a world filled with love, peace and joy. Love means to have a deep, tender fondness and devotion to someone. Be true to yourself and stay devoted to God. Walk in love and live in the life of love and love will find you.

5

RESISTING THE SPIRITS OF LESBIANISM

Sometimes we as women become very impatient when it comes to romance. We get frustrated because it seems like it's going to take forever to find a man, a good man to love us and who we can love in return. So instead of us trusting God to send us the right man, we go outside of the box and try to find a man on our own. This is where a lot of us mess up! When we choose to settle for less all because we want are flesh to feel good and be satisfied for a few seconds, this is what happens. We will get a man who we don't know but only in the bedroom, with no character, no job, no outlook on life, and no spiritual connection with God. Then he breaks our hearts and we are right back to square one again. In this process, our heart is becoming more and more defected with hurt, lies, and deceit. That's why it's important to wait on God to fully equip us for the coming of our prince charming.

Now, for the women who are willing to wait on God to send the right man along, there are some things you must be cautious of. There are a lot of spirits traveling to and fro just waiting to seek whom they may devour. While you wait, you must constantly pray and stay in tune with God and study your bible to keep your mind, heart, spirit, and soul filled with knowledge of Gods word. Don't just kick back and relax, the moment you do that, you will cause the enemy-Satan to make room to move in and take control of your life again. If you don't occupy your time with God, then the enemy-Satan will bring forth the spirit of loneliness upon you and cause you to do other things ungodly that's outside of the will of God. When you keep yourself occupied, you don't have time to focus or worry about other things of unimportance.

There is a difference between being alone and lonely. To be alone is when you are by yourself and no one else is around. Now being alone by choice doesn't bring forth loneliness or boredom, it just means you are by yourself and satisfied with the choice rather long or short term. Now, loneliness is when you are alone not by choice, and you're bored and dissatisfied with it. You long to be with someone or something to occupy your time. Loneliness can become a spirit that can take you to several places that at the time you thought you wanted to go but later regret it. It can cause you to do things with people that you wouldn't normally do and leave you wide open for the kill! When you are lonely, you become so bored that whatever you can find to do with whomever or whatever you will do. This is when your life is headed towards a dangerous path. It leaves your spirit wide open for several other spirits of this wicked world to intervene and attack your body.

One of the spirits I want to talk about is lesbianism. This is a spirit that sneaks up on you so quick that it almost seems natural. It's like you just slide right into it with open arms. See, when your heart has been broken, it leaves a large hole in it, and if you don't ask God to come in and patch it up, it leaves room for any type of spirit to come in and dwell within. There are so many ways that the spirit of lesbianism can come in and so many reasons. A lesbian is a woman who sexually prefers to be with another woman and not a man. Simply said, a lover of oneself. This is not scriptural at all and not pleasing to God. Now a lot of you may be saying to yourselves, I will never become a lesbian. Allow me to give you some reasons why so many other women have become lesbians not by choice.

One of the main reasons so many women have become lesbians is because they have been hurt by so many men and have lost interest in the male gender. Now, if you have been hurt over and over again by a man and your heart feels like it has been ran over by a mat-truck, your heart will become bitter and hardened towards a man or anyone for that matter. So then, the statement comes out of the woman's mouth saying; *I am through with men, I will never date another man as long as I live!* These are the words that have been spoken and brought to life by you, lady. And the worse part is that Satan has heard the words being spoken and has immediately began an attack on your life. Satan says fine, you are through with men, so I'll send you a lady that will love and treat you right. The enemy will begin to plant negative seeds into your spirit and cause you to become physically attracted to the same sex and act out on your emotions. This is one example of how it starts.

As I discussed earlier, the spirit of loneliness is another way to add heat to the spirit of lesbianism. Why? It leaves you open to whatever exciting or interesting that comes your way. Ladies, if we don't have a man and the sexual urge comes rising to our flesh, what is the first thing we do? We will go find our little sex toys and click-ticklers and go in our rooms and play! Now, some of you may say, there is nothing wrong with that? Well, maybe not for the unbelievers, but for the women who are believers in God and are trying to walk the save-walk, there is a lot wrong with it. Listen ladies, why torture yourselves when you can have the real thing? Those sexual toys may arouse you for the moment, but what about afterwards. You will still be alone and in the same situation you were in before. The sexual toys being used produces a spirit, and it's lesbianism. When you use these toys, you are allowing your body to become use to the way it makes you feel and then you won't have a desire for a man, because you've fallen in love with the sex toy!

You will find yourself having no use for a man to satisfy you sexually and then you lose interest in him. Rubbing and feeling on yourself causes you to get used to satisfying yourself and desires and brings forth the spirit of lusting after the same-sex. When you lick and rub on your breasts, you begin to fantasize and desire being with another woman and because you are arousing yourself, you figure you don't need a man when you can satisfy yourself. When you manually operate the sex toys, you have control as to how it goes and you make it move the way you want it to, to satisfy you and then there it goes again, what do I need a man for! Then the next thing you know, you are trying those same moves on another party who is of the same sex. You have brought birth to a defiled, corruptible, and dangerous spirit into your temple. You will be having all types of sexual orgies and having no thoughts of regrets about it.

The third way to invite the spirit of lesbianism in is, vulnerability. My simple definition for vulnerability is to be sensitive and desperate. When you've been hurt and disappointed, sometimes your feelings are so sensitive. When you become this way, especially after being hurt, anyone that shows you an act of kindness or gives you a kind word, you take it to heart. Then you become so desperate for attention and love that you allow yourself to fall into the wrong arms. You made a vow that you will never get involved with another man again, so the devil begins to work out his master plan. So he sends a nice lady your way who greets you with open arms and makes you feel comfortable to talk and open up to her. Then you think to yourself, this lady really listens to me and understands me and my issues. Next, she invites you to her home and shows you truly how she feels and because you miss the caress of a man and the attention, you fall right into the trap and she invites you into the world of corruption, but to you it's a better world in which you've never seen before and you don't want to leave.

The last way to enter into the world of the lesbian lifestyle is from having the seed being planted in you as a young child. A lot of women have been fighting all of there lives trying to prevent from continuously living the lifestyle that was planted in them at a young age. Somewhere a woman as a child, has had a mother, step-mother, grandmother, godmother, aunt, cousin, neighbor, or even a church member to come into their lives and sexually abuse them. And their first sexual experience was with a woman and that's all they know. The seed was planted in them early and all of their lives, they had to fight to live a normal life. Maybe it's one of you reading this book, you tried to date men and even get married but somewhere hidden way deep down the spirit was still there. The marriage was a cover-up, the relationship was to throw people off to keep them from finding out the hidden truth. Whatever the reason may be, it's a spirit that has a strong hold on you and you don't know how to escape. You were married for years, but your husband abused you, you left him and then the spirit that you thought was gone has now been brought back to life.

There is a solution to every problem and just because you were violated as a child doesn't mean you have to continue to bring life to it. You don't have to live that way and pervert your life as well as others. The fight is on and you must fight for what you want and what you believe in. Resist temptation by not going to certain atmospheres, hanging around certain people and allowing yourself to be put into a situation where you may be tempted. I understand that it's a daily struggle being a lesbian or having those feelings, but it doesn't have to be that way. And there is no such thing as being born gay, you were made normal, that is the trick of the enemy. Don't let him fill your mind with such garbage. I don't care how the seed was planted, it originally came from Satan and you have the choice to break the curse in Jesus Name. God is against this type of behavior and he wants you to live a pure and wholesome life. Don't let your issues cripple or paralyze you. Learn to deal with them one by one. If you are struggling with this spirit, go to God in prayer and ask him to deliver you and trust that he will do it. The bible talks a lot about living a sexual immoral lifestyle.

In the book of Genesis Chapter 19 talks about the destruction of the cities, Sodom and Gomorrah. These cities were filled with wicked and defiled people who didn't take heed to Gods warning and continued to live in their sin. Men sleeping with men and women sleeping with women as well as drinking and all sorts of things were going on in that city. In fact, the beginning of this chapter talks about how God sent two angels to Sodom one evening to the place where Lot (Abraham's nephew) was staying. Lot recognized that the two men were angels sent by God but everyone else in the city that saw these men didn't know they were angels. Lot invited them in for a feast and later the house became surrounded by the wicked men of Sodom, old and young asking Lot who were those men. The men tried to force there way into the house, there response to Lot was that they wanted to see the two men so they may know them **carnally.** The two angels grabbed Lot and shut the door and struck the carnal men with blindness. The Lord sent the two angels there to destroy the cities for their wickedness and carnality.

The men were gay, Lot even offered them his two daughters who were virgins, but they refused. The city was so wicked and corrupt that the angels had no choice but to come and destroy. And just like God destroyed those two cities, he will destroy you if you don't get free from those wicked ways. Don't fall into temptation of such a corrupt lifestyle. Don't fill your temple with garbage like this. As I always say, ***IT FEELS GOOD GOING IN, BUT IT'S HELL COMING OUT!***

1 Corinthians Ch3-16-17v

16- Do you not know that you are the temple of God and that the spirit of God dwells in you?

17-If anyone defiles the temple of God, he will destroy him. For the temple of God is holy, which temple you are.

6

A CRY FOR DELIVERANCE

To be delivered from something or someone means to be rescued or set free. There are a lot of women reading this book right now who want to be delivered and set free from some issues in their lives but are afraid to admit it or just simply don't know how. Battered women suffer from so many things such as stress, anxiety, fear, nerve problems, nightmares, low self-esteem and the list goes on and on. No matter what you are dealing with on a personal level, it can effect everything and everyone around you. Your life will continue to be miserable until you admit you have issues and are willing to do something about them. There are a lot of women who don't have a relationship with God-Jehovah, or may even have another God whom they call on or worship. But whoever and whatever you choose to call on - there needs to be a true connection with the real God who can answer your prayers and deliver you from your issues. Religion is another subject, but there is only one true God that can totally set you free from all sin and harm and that's Jehovah, there's no one like him.

There are plenty of nights where you wake up in a cold sweat, thinking about the beatings and abuse. You try to turn over and go back to sleep, but you still see the face of your abuser and the fist that comes brushing toward your face and the loud screams of fear roaring. You go to the doctor to get medicine to help you sleep but it still doesn't help any. Then you turn to the alcohol bottle hoping that you get so drunk that you'll sleep the night away without any interruptions. As the days go by you drink more and more and it becomes a habit. You become addicted to the pills and the alcohol, not realizing that the problem is still going to be there when you awake. Your body becomes immune to both drugs, and then you need to go to a stronger drug to sustain you. You become addicted and you can't get off. This is the time when you need to cry out for deliverance!

The nightmares are horrible and every time you close your eyes, all you can see is your painful past. Every sound you here at night while sleeping, you become frantic thinking it's the abuser trying to come in and finish you off! This is not a good way to live, in constant fear daily. God wants to deliver you from those nightmares and the drugs. Pray that God will send his heavenly angels down to watch over you at night so you can sleep in peace. Peace brings forth a calmness and stillness in your spirit. When you have the peace of God inside of you, you can rest in him knowing that he's got your back and will take care of your every need. God is peace and he will bring a shield of comfort to your life and take away every ounce of fear that is within you.

Low self-esteem is another issue that victims of abuse battle with on a daily basis. A person who suffers from low self-esteem not only deals with it alone, but there are other things that come along with it. Low self-esteem is when you are thinking less of yourself than you should think. When you feel this way about yourself, it brings forth confusion, sadness, loneliness, isolation, even a suicide spirit. When you don't feel loved or appreciated, this spirit can easily come in and take control of you. When someone tells you they love you but do and say all of the wrong things to hurt you- this also adds heat to the fire! This is a serious issue that doesn't need to be taken lightly. The only way to be free from this type of behavior is to know who you are as a person and not allow the thoughts and opinions of others dictate who you are.

Stress is a very serious issue that can damage a person in every way imaginable. When living a chaotic lifestyle filled with drama, it makes life very difficult and hard to bare. The more responsibility that's added on to your plate, the more stress builds up and overwhelms you. Stress also causes strokes, high blood pressure, and heart attacks. Stress can and will kill you if you let it take control. Battered Women go through a lot of stress. It's hard living with someone who's unpredictable, not knowing what mood he will be in when he comes home. You revolve your whole entire world around him by making sure he's satisfied. Living a lifestyle like this keeps you on your toes at all times because you never know when your abuser is going to snap and lose control. This is how stress can come in because you are being forced to do things against your will. Stress can come many ways but the only way to get free from it is to get delivered.

God doesn't want you to stay bound in your troubles, he wants to free you from them. He wants you to cry out for deliverance in every area of your life. Trust God and have faith that he will do it. You may be free from your abusive relationship but the hurt, pain, and shame that it has left behind has caused you to be broken and left with the missing pieces. All God wants you to do is just cry out to him and surrender your life and everything you have to him. Lay down your life for him, set aside the heavy burdens and leave them at the altar of God. He loves you so much that he has given you another chance at living again-freely. Let him set you free from the evil spirits that have surrounded you for so long and the voices of confusion that speak to you over and over again in your head. In order to live your life freely in total fulfillment, ask God to help you after he delivers you from your past issues to not allow you to get entangled into the web of deception again or any other type of temptations. He will help you get on the right track as long as you stay faithful and keep your end of the bargain.

Battered Women also deal with issues concerning the lack of trusting others. It's hard to trust others when the person closest to you lies to you and mistreats you. This causes you to become distant and untrusting towards others. Dealing with domestic violence defects you as a person and everything around you. It changes the way you think, act, and feel towards different situations in your life. You have hardened your heart and built a brick wall around it to keep out the invaders who are only looking out to hurt and destroy you. The truth is, everyone is not out to hurt or destroy you. You need to have the spirit of discernment to distinguish between who is for you and who's against you. Trust brings a bond between people who love and respect each other. Once that trust is broken, it can't be put back together again, because you will always wonder in your mind will that person betray you again.

The bruises, scars, and pains of life has left you wounded and God wants you to be free from the things that are holding you back from growing. You must remember that God is here to help you come out from the state that you're in and move you to a higher dimension in life. Your worst enemy is **YOU!** That's right. You need to get delivered from yourself, your old ways of doing things, the way you think, and your character. You are sitting around settling for less and looking for someone else to blame for your mistakes. God is tired of your complaining, he is saying that you have been down for too long and it's time for you to stop throwing your little pity-party and get up and do something about yourself and your situation. It's your choice as to how you want to live your life. You can live it free in Jesus or live in bondage by Satan-the enemy.

Don't block your blessings, God wants to bless you but you are getting in his way from giving you a life filled with bountiful blessings. If you have come to a point in life where you want to reap the blessings of God, then you need to yield to him. Yielding is taking a quick pause by slowing down and making sure nothing is coming your way before moving forward. When you move forward, God will be waiting straight ahead for you at the end of the crossroad. You have gone through a lonely and dark tunnel and now God wants to show you there is life filled with light at the end of the tunnel. It's not about where you've been it's where you are going. I ask you now to just fall at the master's feet and worship him, tell him how much you love him and how much he means to you. Then begin to tell God what you need him to do in your life and ask him to save you from the snares of the enemy, Satan and his advocates. Begin to ask him to strip you from your sinful ways and deliver you from all evil and the junk that has been deposited into your spirit by the abuser from the beatings on down to the negative words spoken. All God wants you to do is come forth and give him your heart, mind, body, soul, and spirit. He wants to rid you from your painful past and deliver you from the powerful curse of abuse.

7

BREAKING THE GENERATIONAL CURSES OF ABUSE

Every woman and man on this earth comes from a family with issues. There is no such thing as a family who is perfect and has no skeletons in the closet. We are all guilty of doing things in our lives that we aren't exactly proud of. But we need to make sure that we learn from those bad choices and mistakes and make a plea never to do them again. See, whatever bad choices we make in our lives, we must realize that it effects everyone and everything around us good or bad. There are things that our parents did years ago that was bad but it didn't necessarily backfire on them, but the heat from the fire came down to their descendants which are the children they bore. The match that our parents struck to start the fire blew up into flames and kept spreading and spreading until it covered everything in passing. This is how generational curses start, one person strikes the match and the fire keeps burning and traveling and destroying everything it comes in contact with.

To be cursed means to be damned or to have evil brought upon you. It seems like every time something good gets ready to happen in your life, it always blows up in your face. Every time you try to move ahead in life all of a sudden you start going two steps backwards. You try to find your own true identity but others want to identify you as being like your mother or father or another family member that doesn't have a good reputation. When someone curses you they are trying to afflict you with swearing words of deception. Speaking evil against you to keep you from prospering and becoming successful. People who do this are dream killers. They speak against everything positive that you stand for and set out to do. Dream killers always like to remind you of all of the things that you can and cannot do and tell you all of the things you don't have to seek after your goals. Instead of them encouraging you to go after your dreams, they kill them with negative words and reminding you of where you come from to keep you bound to your present situation.

Satan and his advocates wants to make you feel guilty because you want to succeed in life and come out of the depression that you're in. He will send people your way to discourage you and distract you to make you lose focus. He will tell you that just because your grandparents worked in cotton and tobacco fields that you will have to do so as well. Just because your parents dropped out of school at an early age, you will too or your mother had children out of wedlock you will too. That is garbage and a pack of lies! Looking at your family's situations should make you be more determined to live your life better and fight to have more than they had. The only way you won't become successful is if you feed into the lies of Satan and believe what he says. If you choose to follow the footsteps of your family, then and only then will the generational curse work. You can't just say that will never happen to you and stop there, you have to pray for God to deliver you from the family curse and remove the shackles surrounding you. When you see the enemy coming from one direction, you turn around and go in another. Resist the devil and he will flee from you because you aren't giving him any place or room in your life.

There are so many different generational curses that we deal with in every family. Let's discuss one in particular and that's concerning domestic violence and the problems it causes in families and the children who become apart of it. Believe it or not, domestic violence has become apart of a generational curse that destroys families of every race. First of all, it's a spirit of control that comes forth to brainwash whoever that is willing to receive it. Once the controlling spirit is received, it programs the abuser into thinking he is higher than he ought to think. In other words the abuser in his own mind thinks he is God and can not be conquered or defeated. So he then begins to control everything around him and if things don't go his way, he loses his temper and becomes violent. The violent spirit begins to take over and the abuser then retaliates with words and physical abuse and becomes quite destructive. The children are effected as well and sometimes become an easy target for the abuser because they stand as witnesses to the brutal crime being committed. They live in fear because they are being told by the abuser not to tell or this or that will happen. This is not a good way to live.

I'm sure by now you are asking the questions like how does domestic violence become a generational curse? And how did you become apart of it? Well, most battered women either grew up in a household where abuse took place or their abusers grew up in a household where the abuse took place. You became an easy target because you grew up watching your mother get beatings from your father and feeling as if that was the way a woman was suppose to be treated. Maybe you didn't agree to the treatment your mother was getting but because you were in that environment, that spirit fell on you and branded your life. You had a spirit of confusion, low self-esteem, and most of vulnerability covering you and when a man looked at you, that's the first thing he saw. You were so miserable in the household that you were willing to do anything to get out of the house quickly! So you became an easy target for an abusive man on the hunt to entangle you into his web of deception. Trust me, a violent controlling man on a hunt isn't looking for a strong woman who knows who she is, he's looking for a woman who's vulnerable and doesn't know who she is so he can continue to break her down to nothing. This boosts up his ego to make him feel like a king.

There are many women who never grew up in a violent home but somehow they got hooked up with a man who was or just has a violent spirit. As I said earlier, if the woman didn't grow up in a violent home, the abusive mate did or somehow picked up the violent spirit from somewhere else. When young boys grow up in the home with their fathers, they look up to their fathers as role models. They watch their dads wake up every morning and go to work and come home dirty and sweaty from a long hard days work. They observe how their father presents himself as a man and how he handles family situations, as well as how he treats his wife. Boys value the times that are well spent with their fathers. They look up to him as a king and think to themselves how they want to be just like their father when they grow up. When they see how strong, mighty, and powerful their dad is, they strive to be that way as well. Boys need good role models in their lives to follow after, but if their father isn't presenting himself that way, then that makes it hard for the young boy to understand. Everything the young boy sees his father do, he wants to do it too or find another role model to follow which may not be the wise thing to do.

When a young boy grows up watching his father beat his mother, he may not like it or understand it but there is nothing he can do about it. All the young boy can do is just stand there and cry and plead for his father to stop. As the years go by he makes a vow to never hit a woman or treat his wife the way that his father treated his mother. The young boy doesn't realize that the seed of abuse has already been planted in him at a young age. His spirit has been contaminated with that garbage and later as the years go by he begins to believe that the way his father treats his mother is right. He begins to lose respect for his mother because he sees his father has no respect for her. Then when he becomes a young man and starts dating women, he treats them the same way he saw his father treating his mother. He becomes very controlling, demanding and violent when things don't go his way. Since the seed was planted at an early age, it just began to grow and grow because it was continually being fed daily by him watching his father mistreat his mother. When the young boy became an adult he tried hard to fight off the spirit but didn't have the power within himself to win the battle.

The abusive spirit can't come to life unless there is someone that becomes connected to it. If an abuser doesn't have anyone or anything around to pound on then the spirit is at rest hidden from within. This spirit is hidden, most men don't even realize that they have it until the opportune time comes along and they react to it. Just because a boy grows up in a violent home doesn't mean that he has to be that way when he grows up. The truth is in order for him not to become this way is for him to fight and pray on a daily basis for deliverance. As I said before this is a hidden spirit that a man may not even realize he has until provoked. The generational curse starts when the son begins to follow in the footsteps of his father and act out what he sees being done. The son is walking in his father's shadow.

Ladies, that's why it's important for us to really understand why men are abusive and where it comes from. When we have a better understanding of why this happens, we can deal with it a lot better than if we didn't know. Now that we understand more about domestic violence and how it all get's started, we need to fight against it to keep it out of our homes and our lives. As I said in chapter one, it's not the man who is so bad but it's the spirit that's inside of him that causes him to react in such a violent way. We need to pray and come together to make sure that our men of today and tomorrow are no longer defeated by this devouring spirit but come out on top in total victory! Please understand me, I'm not saying to accept this type of behavior and to ignore it. I'm simply saying because of the knowledge you have learned so far you have a better understanding of how to handle the problem and come up with some solutions through prayer and conversation with your partner.

Battered Woman, you have the power to control what happens to you and your life! You don't have to allow this curse to follow you any longer, know your rights and begin to fight. The generational curse stops right now with you. Your daughters will not become victims of such a brutal crime and your sons will not partake in such a terrible act! How can the curse be broken? The answer is through prayer, believing that God will deliver you from this mess and having faith that he hears you and will answer you. Continue to fight and resist the devil and he will flee from you. Know who you are in Jesus Christ and pray over your young children that they will not be affected by this spirit and that the curse is dead and won't return anymore. Pray over yourself and your husband before it's too late and anoint him as yourself and rebuke the spirit. The curse can't live if you continue to fight the good fight of faith. The curses of abuse will hinder you from prospering and destroy you, your kids and everything around you if you don't kill the seed before it grows.

{Prayer}
Father God in Jesus name, May every generational curse of any kind be broken right now. Loose and set free every battered woman. Protect her and her family from danger. And may every evil work done against her fail in Jesus Christ's name. Amen.

8

THE POWER OF A RESURRECTED WOMAN

Every woman has power but the problem is that not all women know how to activate it or use it. The power that we as women have is never discovered until put to the test. Power means a force or energy that can be put to work or to have the ability to control and influence others. Now that you are in a position in life to operate in your power and authority, allow me to share with you what the bible says on walking in power and authority. The book of Romans Chapter 8 talks about being sons and daughters of God through the spirit. Also dealing with the adoption of becoming a child of God through the spirit. The book of Psalms Chapter 82 talks about being gods and children of the most high.

Romans Chapter 8: 14v-17v
14v) For as many as are led by the spirit of God, these are sons of God.
15v) For you did not receive the spirit of bondage again to fear, but you received the spirit of adoption by whom we cry out "Abba Father."
16v) The spirit himself bears witness with our spirit that we are children of God.

17v) And if children, then heirs of God and joint heirs with Christ, if indeed we suffer with him, that we may also be glorified together.

<u>*Psalm Chapter 82: 6v*</u>
6v) I said, "You are gods, and all of you are children of the Most High.

In order to walk in power and authority you must know who you are in Christ and as a woman on the move for him. As long as you allow him to lead and direct you spiritually, everything else will fall into place. Now for the women reading this book who have no relationship with God, allow me to help you walk through this journey of eternal greatness. The first step is salvation. Salvation is the key that will unlock the door to a new life filled with love, joy, peace, happiness and longevity! God will accept you for who you are in whatever state that you're in with open arms, if you'll just come to him. It doesn't matter what you've done in the past, God loves you and is willing and able to forgive you for your past and present sins. The best part about it all is that once he forgives you of your sins, he then casts them all into the sea called "forgetfulness." Wow, who would have thought that there would be a sea called "forgetfulness." In fact, in the book of Isaiah Chapter 43 verses 18-19 says:

18v) Do not remember the former things, nor consider the things of old.
19) Behold, I will do a new thing, now it shall spring forth; Shall you not know it? I will even make a road in the wilderness and rivers in the desert.

God says he will forgive you for all of your wrong doing so therefore you need to forgive yourself as well. There is no need to look back but look to the things that are ahead. The second step is adoption. Now that you've been saved from the sin and carnality of this world, God has adopted you spiritually into his family. God created us in his image and he loves us all but we all cannot say that we are spiritually his children. His children walk in love, loyalty, obedience, righteousness, holiness and integrity. If you are not born again and accepted Jesus Christ as your savior then God is not your father-spiritually and you aren't his child. But if he is your father then you have inherited all that comes from him. You have become an heir of God, which means you have inherited all things that comes from him. God is rich spiritually, financially, and physically-so if he's your spiritual father then everything he has- has now become your inheritance! And to top it off not only are you an heir of God but you have become joint-heirs with his son, Jesus. You are connected with Jesus jointly at the rib! Think about all the power and anointing that Jesus has, all of the miracles and healings he has performed. You can do it too because you are jointly connected with him. When he moves you move, wherever he goes, you go in the spirit.

This is the time when you begin to grow more in God and know who you are in him. Now the third step is sanctification. Sanctification means to be set apart from a person, place, or thing. Simply said, separate yourself from people/places/things who are not of like-mind. You are Gods child now and you no longer belong to the devil or the heathens of this world. Rid yourself from all sin and unrighteousness and whatever habits you once had will return no more if you walk with God whole heartedly. If you are having a hard time breaking free from bad habits, just remember that you are now joint-heirs with Jesus and you can't go where he's not welcomed and you can't do the things that Jesus can't do. The only thing he can't do is sin and fail! You will never see Jesus drunk or high on drugs, nor will you see him fornicating, committing adultery or raising hell! Remember who you are in Christ and as a woman of God. Allow God to fill you with his holy spirit so that you won't have room to sin or contemplate on the unclean things of this world. In order to become powerful in God, you must die to the fleshly desires of this world and come alive in Christ by feeding your spirit with his word.

In the book of Psalms Chapter 82 verse 6, God says we are gods and children of the most high. Now some of you may read this and say it's blasphemous to say that there is any other God but God-Jehovah himself. Now we know there is only one true God and that is Jehovah, but he has a lot of sons and daughters in the spirit who he has adopted as his very own children. God is our father in the spirit and we have inherited all that he has for us because we gave him our lives completely. In saying all of this, he has given us all that he has to offer us, he takes care of us just like our natural fathers would do. So if God has adopted you into his family he has now become your spiritual and legal guardian so he's now responsible for your well-being. His name is GOD! So whatever your last name was when he adopted you has now been changed to the last name, GOD! For example if your name is Susan, your last name has been changed and now it's Susan God! Why? You are his adopted daughter through the spirit and he has changed your last name to something much more powerful and great- you are his little goddess. In the natural realm, a child that is born to a married couple usually carries the last name of the father. So through salvation you are born again and God is now your father so you now have the right to wear his name proud!

Now before we go any further, don't start walking around claiming you are the female messiah! That's not what this means. God-Jehovah is the ***BIG-G*** and you are the ***little-g!*** He's the biggest and the greatest and there is no one like him. God has claimed you as his daughter in the spirit and named you his little goddess of light. Grab hold to God because being connected to him makes you connected with all things in the spirit. God has several links. Once you get connected with God, you have access to his anointing, knowledge, wisdom, love, joy, peace, prosperity, dominion power, and most of all his son, Jesus Christ. You have been chosen by God to do a perfect work in his will. He saw something in you that you didn't realize was there. God knew there was potential in you and he came to bring it out from underneath and bring it to the light. God will take the most feeble person and change them into something great! Don't focus on the old you and how you used to be, focus on what God has made you become in him. Your old life was filled with sin, shame, and drama. When you came to God you brought all of that junk with you standing before him but you made the choice to leave it all at the altar of Gods throne and not take it back with you. There comes a time when you must live and die. To feed the flesh means to give it what it wants by satisfying your fleshly desires. The flesh will never die if it's being fed daily with earthly lusts. However, if you don't eat food, your flesh will starve to death. If you don't drink water your flesh will dehydrate and eventually die due to starvation and dehydration. In the spiritual since, if you don't feed flesh with sin, it will surely die and when it dies that leaves room for the spirit of God to step in and take control. You feed your spirit with the word of God and through prayer, praise, worship, and strengthening your spirit through fasting. When you accept Jesus Christ as your savior, you yield to him totally and your flesh dies when the holy spirit takes control. You are dead to sin and now you have to be brought back to life in Jesus. This process is called the Resurrection.

Jesus died on the cross and was laid in a tomb. Jesus arose from the grave and on the third day- he was resurrected from the dead. When Jesus had risen from the dead, he was completely restored and more powerful than ever. He didn't lose anything, but gained so much! Ladies, you have been resurrected from the old life you had, from the death that sinned caused to kill you, and from your broken relationships. Now that you have risen from the dead, God has given you power to live and walk in authority. Before Jesus descended into heaven he left his people a very special gift and that is the gift of the holy spirit. He left the holy spirit as a comforter, helper, leader and guider to all mankind to teach us and show us all things in the spirit. Now that you have that gift, put it to good use. Anytime you need the spirit of God to surround you just call and the holy spirit will be by your side instantly.

There is power in a resurrected woman of God. God has spared your life because he has chosen you for this day and time to help set the captives free. Battered Woman, you have a story to tell, a testimony to share, and souls to witness to. God saved you because he knows he can trust you with his anointing and his holy power. He allowed you to go through all of the hell you have experienced because he was preparing you for something greater. He knew you would survive because you are strong, he knew you would keep fighting until the battle was finally won and he got the glory out of it all. God has equipped you with his dominion power so you can take this world by storm and make your mark. He didn't let you die because he saw a very special gift in you that he knew would be of value to the people in the world. God can't use a lifeless vessel nor can he use a damaged or defected one. He had to strip you and kill your flesh so he can resurrect you into a powerful and mighty woman of God. A Godly woman has power to heal and help deliver the souls who are sick in sin and lost. A powerful woman knows who she is and where she is going and doesn't depend on a man or others to define who she is or dictate to her how she should live her life.

When you are walking in authority, you call the shots and you learn how to take control of your day and the atmosphere around you. You are a leader not a follower, above and not beneath, and the head not the tale. People may not agree with your ways of doing things nor may they be very fond of you, but one thing is for sure, they will respect you. A woman who has been resurrected is almost like being reincarnated. The old body dies but when resurrected, it is in a new form and body. The new body is in effect and doesn't operate the same. The old weak body is now strong, the lying tongue is now filled with truth, the foul language is now filled with a praise to God and the heart and mind has been made brand new. People wouldn't even recognize you if your facial appearance didn't look the same. See, when you die to sin and awaken to salvation, you should have a whole new attitude and persona about yourself. People should be able to look at you and see a change and when in your presence, they should feel at peace and know the spirit of God is within you.

When you are walking in power others around you should be able to feel it, sense it, see it, and experience it. Whoever and whatever that comes in contact with you should also be walking in power as well, the fire has to keep burning. Don't hang around anyone that is weak and has lack of faith, such things as this can cause your fire to be put out. It's very important that you be careful of the company you keep. Surround yourself around people who are strong and powerful and have a lot of faith. The more you hang around people who are like you and stronger than you, it keeps you motivated to become the best you can be in all areas of your life. Power comes from God and he gives it to the ones who are worthy and hungry for it and most of all who he can trust with it. If your intensions aren't good, then he won't bless you with power and authority. Power and authority isn't for you to walk around mistreating and hurting others or for your selfish gain. It simply helps you to learn how to defeat the enemy and your adversaries by knowing who you are and that God has your back and with him you will win every battle and climb every mountain that has been placed in your path.

Battered women must rise from the hard fall of life. Don't just lie there and wait for people to pity you and pick you up, get up and dust yourself off and keep moving. Learn how to take control of your life and be that successful woman that God has called you to be. It doesn't matter what you've lost, the important thing is that with God you will gain everything you've ever wanted. Walk in the power and authority that you possess and go get your life back girl! Rise my sister, stand up and rise for the day has come for you to claim what is yours and go after your destiny. Realize that you are a daughter of promise and all that God has for you. Rise up from the grave of sin and shame and be descended into a higher place where God wants to place you. There is power in the resurrected woman, for she is like a space shuttle ready to go into orbit. Strive for greatness and success in all areas of your life. Be all you can be girl, for you are now marching in the army of the most high God! Last but not least, when you have the power of God, you control your life through him and how you handle certain situations. You are bold and undefeated. Whatever you speak out of your mouth, shall be and whatever you touch shall be blessed. Every ground you walk on, shall be blessed and prosperous. There shall be no sickness or diseases among you nor shall their be poverty. For there is power and authority in a resurrected woman of God in Jesus Name. Amen!

9

THE MAKING OF A VIRTUOUS WOMAN

In the bible, the book of Proverbs Chapter 31 verses 10-31 talks about the characteristics of a virtuous woman. She is a woman of integrity who is very strong and powerful. A woman of peace, holiness, righteousness and purity. The heart of a virtuous woman is filled with goodness, love, compassion, and forgiveness. She works hard and strives for excellence and takes great pride in her duties as a wife and a mother to her children. For she lends a helping hand to those who are in need and her works are not done in vain. She makes sure that her household is taken care of properly and her husband and children aren't in need of anything. A virtuous woman knows who she is, what she wants, and knows where she's going in her life. She puts her family first and herself last. She sets a mark of high standards for herself and is known in the gates of the city as being a blessed woman of God as well as her husband and children.

This all sounds so easy, but we as women have to go through some major challenges in our lives in order to become a strong and virtuous woman. The book of Proverbs discusses the life of a virtuous woman in present tense but I can only imagine the hell she went through in order to reach that level of grace. A virtuous woman has to go through some twisters, hurricanes, tornados, and earthquakes in her life before she can ever see the sunshine with the rainbow of promise around it. She also has to go through a process and preparation before she can reach the level of virtuosity. The problem with a lot of us is that we want to be beautiful, popular, rich, and want everything done in a hurry. God doesn't rush when he is doing a great work in our lives, he takes his time. We want the blessings from God but not willing to pay the price for them. In every blessing received, there is a price we have to pay for it. Nothing comes easy in life, rather it's in the spiritual or natural realm.

There is virtuosity in every woman but it has to be activated in order to be used. For example, you can have an A.D.T alarm system in your home and the sign hanging outside in the yard, but until turned on or activated, it's no good. That's how virtuosity works, a woman has to learn how to activate and use it in her daily walk of life. The process starts as a seed being planted inside of you as your mother was carrying you in her womb. The moment you were born the seed began to taper off and grow day after day. Now in order for the seed of virtuosity to be birthed out, it has to be properly nurtured. A mother should be a little girls role model as a child growing up. A little girl watches everything her mother does and tries to mock the way she talks, walks, and dresses. The mother is setting the standard for how her daughter should act. The point is, the virtuous seed has to be properly nurtured by your mother feeding you positive food for your soul and spirit. If the mother is teaching her daughter how to talk, walk, dress, act, and carry herself as a lady, then as she matures it will be instilled in her. It's up to your mother to empower you daily with wisdom so you can realize the powerful virtuous woman you are.

Now, I do realize that there are some women out there who weren't raised by their mothers. Some of you had to raise yourselves and survive the best way you could. There are also some of you who had a mother around, but she didn't have a loving and nurturing spirit. She didn't know how to love or receive love from others because she didn't have that when she was a child. But for those who had a loving mother, you know how it feels to be told you are loved, honored, and appreciated. You can remember the talks your mother gave you about the birds and the bees and how to carry yourself as a lady at all times. Those are the tender moments you can truly cherish for a lifetime. For the women who were not properly loved and nurtured, I want you to know you are special in Gods eyes and loved, honored, and cherished. You are a virtuous woman and it's time for you to birth it out and bring life to it.

When a woman is pregnant her body goes through a lot of changes. She has to carry the baby for nine months before birth. Now during this time, she has to be very careful with the things she does to insure the safety of her baby. While the mother is pregnant three things can happen, she can have a miscarriage, abortion, or a healthy birth. In the spiritual realm, you are pregnant with your seed of virtuosity. You have been carrying it and unsure about what to do with it or how to care for it on your own. If not careful, you can have a miscarriage which means you are giving birth to a baby that's not fully developed enough to live. The baby was born premature and too early before it's proper time. In the spiritual realm, this is a woman who is impatient and wants to rush the process of birthing her virtuous seed. She wants to get the blessing in a hurry so she can shine before man and the world! Giving herself credit for her works and boasting and bragging before the world who she is, what she has, and who she's helped along the way. She's pretending to be a strong and powerful woman trying to operate on a premature seed that is dead. Nothing she does will last because there is no life behind it, no promise. Be careful not to rush and step out too soon because you will make a mess of things and everything you do will blow up in your face. Carry your virtuous seed the whole term, so when God is ready for you to give birth, it will fully be developed to operate properly.

Abortion means the birth of an offspring before it's developed enough to live. Also means failure to succeed or fruitless. My definition of abortion is simply one word; **MURDER!** When you abort your virtuous seed you have killed a major part of yourself without knowing it spiritually. You have killed an innocent part of yourself that never had a chance to flourish. When someone aborts a baby, they are just thinking in the present terms, not the future. There are after affects and defects that come after a woman has an abortion. They have to deal with all kinds of emotional and health issues, and most of all their guilty conscience. Rather you realize it or not, to abort and innocent life, you curse yourself. That's why so many women who have had abortions before can't have anymore children or keep having miscarriages. When a woman aborts her virtuous seed, she does it with a cold and selfish heart. She thinks of no one but herself and doesn't realize the seriousness of it. Sometimes she can kill the seed by the way she thinks, because she was never loved or raised by her mother, she thinks she can never give love to anyone else. The words she speaks can kill her seed by negativity and cursing her life. What is in you will come out of you and if hatred, selfishness, deception, and wickedness is in you then that's what will come out of you. A miserable person can easily abort the seed without knowing it, but if you allow Satan to feed you negative words and make you feel you don't need your virtuous seed- you will kill it. Aborting your seed means you are also interrupting the plans of God. Whatever he had planned for you that was great, you just killed it.

Giving birth to your virtuous seed means you have carried it full term and allowed God to nurture it properly. You didn't rush God, you allowed him to prepare you for the coming of your seed. You are walking in the fullness of virtuosity! You are talking, walking, acting, dressing, and living like the true virtuous woman that God has called you to be. The nine months of being pregnant you were going through a process to prepare you for what is yet to come. You went through some heartache, sickness, pain, hurt, low self-esteem, rejection, and persecution. God allowed you to go through that to make you strong and become the virtuous woman that you are today. If you never go through anything in life, you won't know anything about survival or how to make it through those tough moments in life. This is all part of the making of a virtuous woman. You have to go through some changes but when you finally give birth to your virtuous baby, you will have bundles of joy all around you.

In Proverbs Chapter 31:10, it says a virtuous woman's worth is far above rubies. Now if you know anything about jewelry you know that rubies (real rubies) are very expensive, and to know that God has classified you as being above the price of rubies is more than any woman can ask for. Verse 11 says her husband safely trusts her and has no lack of gain. When you are a good and honest woman your husband knows he can trust you with all that he has and will lose nothing but gain a lot. Now this applies to the women who have saved husbands, if your husband is abusive he won't look at you in the way that a saved husband would. The 12th verse says you will do good by him and not evil all the days of your life. This means no matter how bad your husband may treat you, continue to do good by him and you will be blessed, two wrongs don't make a right. Verse 13 says you work with your hands willingly. Means you don't mind getting your hands dirty and working hard to care for your family and verse 14 says you bring food from afar- you will go the extra mile to get what you need to provide for your family. The 15-16 verse says you will arise while it's night to provide food for your family, simply said you will take care of the household while the family is resting.

All of the scriptures in Proverbs are very important but the verses I'm discussing are very important. Moving down to verse 20, it says a virtuous woman extends her hand to the poor and reaches out her hands to the needy, this is self explanatory. Verse 25 says strength and honor are her clothing, meaning she's a strong woman who is honored and respected for what she does and her strength is seen before God and man. The 26th verse says she speaks wisdom and on her tongue is the law of kindness. She is a woman of wisdom and knowledge and when she opens the doors of her mouth, she speaks truth and kindness to all mankind not lies, rumors and negativity. Verse 27 says she watches over her household and doesn't eat bread from idleness; meaning she makes sure her house is in order and in need of nothing and doesn't take anything from anyone who's not honest. Verse 28 says her children shall rise up and call her blessed and her husband also shall praise her. Her children love and respect her for what she has done for them and her husband praises her for her great works she has done for him, the children and others. Verse 29 says you exceed in all you do in your great works for God. Verse 30 says charm is deceitful and beauty is passing, but a woman who fears the Lord shall forever be praised. Finally, verse 31 says Give her the fruit of her hands, and let her own works praise her in the gates. A virtuous woman shall reap the fruits of her labor and because of her works she shall be praised because it was done from her heart of grace.

A virtuous woman doesn't have to pretend to be something she's not, nor does she have to be put on a pedestal before man to be defined. She knows who she is and has the heart of God and in all she does she does it from the heart. The making of a virtuous woman is a long process but it's well worth the wait. It's important for all virtuous women to be Christ-like and surround themselves with positive people who's after the same things they are. Virtuous women are like missionaries, they reach out to the communities to help others who are in need and get together and pray for others to be healed, delivered, and set free. They don't operate out of flesh, but always the spirit. They don't live their lives according to mans way of doing things, they go by the word of God. Also, they love their husbands and are faithful to them and make sure all of their needs are met as well as the children. They don't worship their husbands, they just love them and make them feel like a king on top of the hill! For every virtuous woman there is a virtuous man.

10

THE FIGHT IS ON!

For years women have been ignored, disrespected, cheated, and belittled. We have been brainwashed into thinking that we are less than a man and that our place was only in the kitchen and the bedroom. In the early years it was disgraceful for a woman to speak out without the approval of a man or higher superior which was of the male gender. If a woman worked on a job and had the same position as a man, he got paid more. The sad thing is, this still happens today. Men get paid more than women and recognized first for the same works that a woman does. Our early mothers have fought the good fight of faith and struggled with blood, sweat, and tears to get us where we are today. Even though there are mountains we have to climb and bridges we still have to cross, we still have more opportunities to succeed now than ever before. There is no excuse as to why women of any race should not be able to succeed in life and have the same opportunities as men. Our early mothers had to fight for what they believed in and so do we. Ladies, the **FIGHT IS ON!**

All of us have goals that we want to achieve and higher standards that we have set for ourselves to meet. Even though we strive for excellence in all that we do, we still have personal battles that we have to overcome in our lives. Personal fears, hidden demons, and battles with the mind has caused us to lose focus on the destiny that lies ahead of us. Satan is fighting hard against women because he knows that we are a powerful force. There is nothing like getting women together in prayer and fasting. Women praying together can destroy yolks and burdens. Our prayers can reach heaven and back ending in a result of a powerful breakthrough. We are the apples of Gods eye and he hears our earnest prayers, especially the prayers of the righteous women of God. Satan knows the weak spots of a woman and he tries to work hard to tear and break her down in that area. That's why a woman has to fight and protect what is rightfully hers. She has to put on the breastplate of righteousness to protect her heart from the fiery darts of the enemy.

God doesn't need any coward soldiers. A coward is someone who doesn't have a backbone, afraid to stand up to others and face their fears. God needs a woman who will be strong and bold that he can use to perform his great works. Not only do you need to be strong for God, but for yourself as well. See, when you are a coward you will settle for anything and take whatever comes your way. You will let people run and step all over you but a strong warrior for God will stand up for what's right and defend themselves. The same thing goes with Satan, you can't be afraid of him because people says he's ugly and has big red horns! You have to smell the enemy when he's coming and be prepared to meet him head on and rip his head off. You can't defeat the devil in your own strength but with God's help and his holy spirit inside of you, you can and will win. Even in the natural world, you can't conquer your adversary alone, you need help and strength to do so. It's time for you to stop walking around in fear and stand up and face your opponent face to face. There were times when you would get into a fight or altercation and not even understand why. All you did was just fight back rather you won or lost without a cause. It's time for you to stand up for what you believe in and fight for what's right in your heart. You have reached a time in your life where God wants to equip you for the battle of a lifetime and this time it's for a real cause.

Battered Woman, you have gone through so much hell and turmoil in your life, you have lost so many battles but God is ready for you to win the war! He wants you to lose the coward spirit, and learn to face your enemies head on. The coward spirit came upon

60

you in your abusive relationship because every time you tried to fight back you lost the battle. So you decided to give up and stop standing up for what you believe in because you felt you didn't have a chance at winning. In fact, a lot of times you pretended to be knocked out on the floor because you knew if you stood up, it would be hell to pay. You are no longer a punching bag and God has brought you too far to leave you and now he wants to train you how to fight. Not to be violent but for everything you have worked so hard for and learning how to fight to keep it. Look at all the chapters you have read so far. You have learned how the spirit of violence starts in a man and how you can break free from it. You also have learned how to love yourself and start new beginnings without the junk in your life. As well as being delivered from the curses of abuse and the perverted thoughts of lesbianism (just in case it crossed your mind) and becoming a powerful resurrected woman of God. Now it's down to the wire, now you know how to activate your virtuosity and how to walk in it. So God wants to teach you how to **fight!**

Before a boxer fights, he has to go through training for weeks. It's not an easy process, he has to get up early in the morning and run and exercise. He has to go on a strict diet and eat the right foods. He even has to psych himself out. What I mean by this is that he constantly has to tell himself how bad he is and that no one can beat him, he's the greatest fighter alive! A fighter has to totally change the way he thinks and feels about himself and his opponent. A lot of work and preparation goes into this sport and it will certainly show if you haven't been working out properly or training as you should have. The moment the boxer gets into the ring, it's on! No remorse, no apologies, just straight kickin' butt! To make a long story short, somebody will win and the other will lose. The fighter who wins is the person who has been properly trained and has studied his opponent enough to know when to move in for the kill. The winner allows his opponent to tire himself out early in the beginning of the match. This way he can catch him at his weakest point and make a move for the final knockout! When you catch your opponent at his weakest point, you just keep fighting and never stop until they give up. That's when you know you have won the battle. As in the spiritual realm, the devil will keep fighting you over and over again with all he has until you decide to get up and fight back. Once you fight back with the word of God and with your praise and worship- the devil can't win, he will lose. The devil can't stand hearing the name of Jesus, so he has to flee far from you.

When the Lord is training you to be a fighter, he will have you getting up early in the morning in prayer. You won't even know why or who you are praying for but he will have you praying. When he does this it means that he is preparing you for what is to come, rather good or bad. He also wants you to pray to interrupt the plans of the devil from prospering in your life. The Lord sees farther than what you can see, so he prepares you ahead of time through prayer. The Lord also prepares you by allowing trials and tribulations to come in your life. The devil has no power unless God gives it to him, he has no room to disrupt your life unless God allows him to. The reason God allows the devil to bring forth trials is only to make you strong. Trials come to help build up your faith and to teach you patience in waiting on God. Going through trials are like a boxer lifting his weights during weight training. The more trials you have, the more weight that is carried upon your shoulders. The only way the burdens can be lifted is through prayer, praise, worship, and strong faith to believe that God will lift every burden from your life. Gods word gives you strength to lift the heavy burdens off your shoulders.

Another way that God trains you to fight is through studying his word. The bible is filled with knowledge that will help you make it through everyday life. The word is what strengthens you in your weak areas and guides you when you can't see your way out of your situations. It's imperative to study God's word because when the wiles of the devil come forth to confuse your mind with false doctrine you need the word inside of you to ward them off. No root, no fruit! By this I mean the word is the root and when you allow the root to grow inside of you then it flourishes into a full harvest of the fruits of the spirit. Someone can curse you out using profane language, but you can curse them out with the word of God in Jesus' name. People can speak derogatory against you but you can speak to them in a kind and positive manner. When the word is in you, you feel like an undisputed champion in the boxing ring. The reason I say this is because for every liar, back-stabber, gossiper, peace breaker, jealous, and envious person, there is you standing fully equipped to knock them out with the word of God. You will stand flat footed and let them know that you aren't going to tolerate that junk in your life or atmosphere. The word is what keeps you in perfect peace and keeps you in tune with God.

God wants to equip you spiritually as well as in the natural for the outside world. You can't make it in this world today without God or having any knowledge of him. In this world today, it's every man for himself. No one cares about the thoughts and feelings of others, it's all about the individual. Listen, you have been down too long and it's time for you to stand up and fight for your rights and let your voice be heard. As I've said earlier, your past is your past and now you are living in the future which can be very promising if you apply yourself. Don't you dare throw in the towel or your boxing gloves. It's time for you to fight to make it into the big leagues. Fight for your success, prosperity, your family, and your blessings in life. Keep on fighting for love, joy, peace, happiness, restoration, and deliverance in your life. Girl fight for your life! Don't just throw one punch and stop, you've got to keep on punching until you knock out every demon, stronghold, adversary, dream killer, root-worker, and backstabber out in your life! Girlfriend, you've got to get ugly for the Lord and praise your way out of the valley of deception and depression. Worship unto the Lord until you get behind the veil of promise.

You must become a spiritual bully to scare off the devil's imps. No one ever bothers a bully because of the reputation that he or she has. A bully is known for beating people up and getting whatever he or she wants. A spiritual bully is the same way, you must learn how to make demands and take what you want in Jesus' Name and let the enemy know he can't take it back. You must speak with authority and know that you are wearing the breastplate of righteousness and shall not and will not be defeated. Because you are walking in authority and covered under the blood of Jesus Christ, people can see the power and strength upon you and will know that you are not to be tampered with. A bully gets much respect from the wimps and doesn't have to worry about being messed with. Everybody knows the name of a bully in town, well the devil and his imps should know yours and run at the sound of your name! You my lady, must get yourself in a place where others can fear you as well as the God in you. I'm not saying to bully people in the natural but let people know that you are undefeated because God has got your front and your back. Let them know that God lives in you and you are the head and not the tale, above and not beneath and if anyone tries to mess with you they have to go through the father first. And you know what the response will be.

You are no longer cast down but highly lifted up. Learn how to fight for your life and all that's in it and you will always come out on top as long as God is your trainer. Not only do you have to fight to become a winner but to remain the undisputed champion. Fight to stay away from negativity, low self-esteem, your past, and tainted atmospheres. Keep on fighting the good fight of faith and beat down your fears, doubts, confusion of the mind, the demons of your past and most of all your worst enemy- you. Remember the devil may have won some of the battles in your life but he surely won't win the war. Put on your boxing gloves girl, because the "**<u>FIGHT IS ON</u>.**"

11

THE SEASONS OF LIFE

Life has many twists and turns but if you follow the straight and narrow path in which God has laid out for you, you can't go wrong. While traveling on the journey of life you will see, experience, and learn things that will help you in your future to come. It's good to travel and see places you've never seen before and experience the life of many different cultures and ethnicities. That's the way it works with the four seasons of life. You are able to witness and see the transformations from one season to another. The four seasons of life are winter, spring, summer, and fall. Every single person living on this earth goes through the seasons of life. Just like the weather changes, so do we and the atmosphere around us. We are effected by the changes of the weather and depending on the climate determines our mood. Believe it or not, the weather does determine ones mood swings and how they feel at that moment. Every season brings forth a change in your emotions rather good or bad, happy or sad. Just like the wind flows through the air in four different directions, we as a people experience the four winds of life. By this I mean, we are sometimes up (north), sometimes down (south), sometimes right (east), and sometimes wrong (west).

In order to pass the tests of life you must be willing to study it by reading the word of God. The bible tells you everything you need to know concerning living holy. For every problem you have in your life, there is a solution found in the bible for it. There will be times when you will fail the tests of life. There will also be times when you will fall into fleshly temptations. When this happens don't just lay down and wallow in your sin, but get up, dust yourself off, repent unto God and keep on moving. The way to overcome your failure is to learn from your mistakes and know what precautions to take to prevent yourself from doing it again. Throughout the seasons of life you will go through major transitions. Spiritually speaking, you will change with God's seasons in his timing. The important thing to remember is, each season elevates you to a higher level. In between the changing of seasons you will lose some things. Just like in the autumn season the leaves turn brown and yellow and eventually fall off the tree, that's what happens in your transitioning period. Even though you will lose some things in your life, you will also gain more to make up for what you've lost in the last season. Each season takes you higher and the things you've lost didn't matter because they were a hindrance to you anyway. Whatever is unclean or unworthy in the eyesight of the Lord can't crossover with you in your new seasons of life.

The season of winter is a time when it's very cold, dry, brisk, and at times very dreary. The winter winds are so strong and powerful and lures you to stay inside of the house to keep warm. Even though winter can be very cold, dry and depressing, it can also be very cozy, relaxing and very romantic. It just depends on how you look at it. Some people love winter because it's cool and fun while playing in the snow. On the other hand it can become a hindrance for people who love to travel. The spiritual side of winter is not at all fun under any circumstance. When you are going through the winter season of life, it means you are at a stand still in your life. Because of your disobedience to God, you have caused a strong wind to come forth and blow your blessings away. The plans that God has for your life and the blessings have all been put on hold for a season. You've missed out on the first opportunity of your blessings due to procrastination and being stubborn. God has placed you in a winter season to keep you still long enough so he can show you some things. As long as you are busy, you won't have time to listen to his voice or catch the signs.

During your winter season God shows you your true self. He reveals to you who you are and the areas of your life that needs changing and deliverance. When he brings snow in your life, he's trying to kill the germ of sin that's trying to destroy your life. When he brings an ice storm your way he's freezing your mind from thinking carnal thoughts, your heart from feeling wickedness, and stopping you from falling into temptation. Even though in your winter season you are at a stand still, God is performing his transitional process in you to prepare you for your next season. Cold atmospheres causes you to withdraw from it with a feeling of numbness. You won't stay in a cold place very long without any heat. For example you can feel the cold spirit of a person who dislikes you or who has been speaking negatively about you. The moment you walk into their presence, you begin to feel the coldness and resentment that makes you feel uncomfortable. In your winter season God makes you uncomfortable with your present living situation. He wants to push you so hard that you will want to change from your wicked ways. He will continue to have you in the winter season of life as long as you continue to live a life that's contrary to his word. Remember in the winter everything stops growing and flourishing. The grass stops growing, the trees are leafless, and the flowers have no bloom. Simply said, in your winter season of life you are at a stop sign waiting for God to move all of the traffic of sin out of your way so you can move to the next level.

After you have passed the test of winter by deciding to move "self" out of the way so God can elevate you, you can move on to the next season, which is spring. Spring is such a lovely season because everything shines, blooms, and grows. The April Showers rains down the blessings from God to water the seeds he's planted in your life to bloom to a full harvest. Spring time is harvest time. Find some good soil and plant your seed into the ground and begin to water it daily with the word of God and watch it grow. You have had so many bad seeds poured into your soil of life that it's hard for you to believe that you can actually grow a fruitful harvest. A battered woman has a mixture of good soil with bad seeds. In the past you have allowed your abuser as well as others to plant bad seeds into your good soil. The outcome was a fruitful harvest full of rotten fruit filled with the wiggle worms of sin and deception. Now God wants to turn it around for you and make your crop a full bloom of fresh fruit with a scent of holiness and righteousness. God is bringing life back to you and your present situation. He's adding a smile to your frown and removing the darkness from your life. There is a dark and dull spirit that God will remove from your life in your spring season. You will begin to feel the breath of the Lord upon you that brings a fresh anointing upon your life and spirit. In the spring flowers open up and bloom, the grass grows so beautiful and green and everything comes to life again. You are reborn again in your spring season and all things in your life become new.

Summer is a very hot and humid season. Also the season for excitement and adventure. Summer is a time for action and brings on the heat in every situation in your life. Summer brings forth the birthing of your promise. When something is hot, you can't hold on to it, you must let it go. When you drink something and it's too hot, you must spit it out! Summer in the spirit realm pushes you to birth out your blessings of promise. The heat of God is upon you so strong that you can't stand it. Everything that you have been praying for and believing in God for has got to happen because of your faith and belief. When you are hot, you sweat. Well, God wants you to work up a sweat of prayer, praise, and worship for him so he can tear down the walls that's been holding up your blessings. He wants you to stop holding on to what is dead and get on fire for him! Summer in your spirit brings on the heat of praise and deliverance. It pushes you to go forth in Jesus' name. A lot of times we won't move unless God gives us a little heat to cause us to move quickly. Summer helps you get on fire for God and carry out his plan.

The fall or autumn season of life is my favorite because everything changes right before your eyes. The leaves turn yellow, brown, and pink. The birds are soaring high in the air and everything is so beautiful and colorful. The amazing thing about the fall season is exactly what it says everything falls off and then later starts over again. The spiritual side of this is God is stripping you from all the junk in your life. He's ridding you from all the wrong people, places, and things in your life. Everything bad falls off and leaves you naked before the Lord which causes him to clothe you with his blessings of promise. God strips you only to rebuild and reconstruct you again so he can smooth out the rough edges. In this season nothing can follow you that's unworthy, this is your season of transition. Out with the old and in with the new. Be thankful for the four seasons of life and cherish every one.

12

VICTORIOUS LIVING

In order to have victory in your life you must defeat the devil by winning your battles and overcoming your struggles. Once you move to a higher dimension in God he will allow you to experience the finer things in life and show you all of the things that you've never seen before. To be victorious means you can conquer anything or anyone that comes your way. You are the head and not the tale, above and not beneath. Blessings come into your life and cause you to be joyful and full of peace. Having the victory means that everyday of your life you are walking in abundance and total restoration. God will set you up high above all so that your enemies will be looking up to you, meanwhile you're looking down at them.

Living a life of victory publicly broadcasts your life to all who see you. People wonder how you got your nice home, new car, fat bank account, and a job that pays you exceptionally well. They don't understand how you left from the land of not enough to the land of having more than enough. You were poor and struggling to make ends meet. You also had to deal with an abusive relationship along with emotional issues that damaged you severely. People don't understand how you got to this point, so they begin to player-hate on you and speak negatively against your blessings. Before you can ever make it to **"Victory Boulevard"** you will have to drive pass **"Sin Street,"** and travel on through **"Temptation Avenue."** Then pass three more streets called; **"Hypocrisy Street," "Backbiting Boulevard," and "Envy Street."** Then you must merge over to the left lane and go down **"Long-suffering Lane," "Persecution Avenue," and "Trials and Tribulations Boulevard."** Once you have driven pass all of these areas you will finally make it to your rest stop!

In case you don't understand what I'm saying, allow me to explain. People who are on the outside looking into your life through a glass window are wanting your goods. They see how you are prospering and how blessed you are and they want to get a piece of the action. They don't want or appreciate the things they have, they want your stuff! They just think you are an overnight success. The truth is, they didn't see you when you were down and out, stressed, depressed, on the verge of suicide, going through physical and verbal abuse, nor did they see the tears you cried and how you walked the floors all night long in prayer. They just see you at your present level of grace. You had to pray and fight to get to where you are today and it wasn't easy, in fact the road was long and hard but you made it because of your determination. It's not easy getting on that victorious path of life, you have to go through some hell and turmoil in your life to get to that point. People always want the blessings but never want to go through anything to get it. It is a price to pay for everything you get from God. Sometimes it hurts but most of the time it feels darn good!

Nothing comes easy from God. He makes you work hard for everything you ask him for. When you ask him for peace in your life, he will allow you to go through some havoc in your life so when he gives you the peace, you will appreciate it. When you ask him for faith, before he gives it to you, he will allow you to go through some hellish storms to see if you will be patient enough to wait on him and trust that he will bring you out. Also waiting to see if you will praise him in the midst of your storm. Even when you ask God for spiritual strength, he will allow the enemy to come in and pile so many burdens onto your shoulders that you are about to tip over. You will become overwhelmed and stressed out but if you can prove to God that you can endure the pain and suffering, he will build you up where you've been torn down. If you ask him to deliver you from your bad habits, he will definitely make you work. God will make you sweat! The deliverance prayer is hard because you have to do most of the work. You have to be determined that you are going to stop doing whatever it is you are doing and once God sees you are serious about your change, then he will grant your request.

The problem is we want things to happen too quick and then when it doesn't we give up. Listen, your road wasn't the smoothest, it was very rocky, but with the help of the lord you got there. Live your life to the fullest and don't you let your past dictate your future. Don't allow others to make you feel guilty because you are living a blessed life. You are no longer a victim of abuse but now a forever victor in Jesus' Name. You deserve to live a life of joy and peace after all the hell you have been through. Don't take for granted the blessings that God has given you and the lessons you've learned. Don't regret the fact that you went through an abusive relationship, you may not see it now but later on you will see that it has helped you become smarter, stronger, and more alert. Learn from your mistakes and don't bring your past into your future.

You are a winner and a very successful woman of God. Everything you touch shall be blessed and all of your descendants after you shall be blessed as well. Remember God loves you and this is your time and your season to be blessed! My best wishes go out to you and your brand new life filled with victory. May God bless every woman reading this book and may your hearts be touched by the words of wisdom in this book. I'm encouraging every woman who is battling with physical abuse to seek help quickly. If you are married, both of you need to get help together and if he's not willing to change-pack your bags my sister and go! But if you can work it out by all means do. A family that prays together stays together. Continue to travel on your journey of peace and victorious living!

ABOUT THE AUTHOR

Janella Purvis is a gifted writer who has published her first book, "A Battered Woman's Guide To Victorious Living." She mentors teenagers on the importance of education and young women on single-motherhood, relationships and spirituality. Also enjoys doing missionary work by helping others who are in need and participating in fundraisers for shelters for battered women.

www.ingramcontent.com/pod-product-compliance
Lightning Source LLC
Chambersburg PA
CBHW030411290526
45785CB00004B/1964